An Evolved, Professing Christian Man™

My Experience of Failures, Trials, Faith, Victories and Love

A Memoir

BYRON DEMERY

Copyright ©2020 by Byron Demery

All rights reserved. No part of this publication may be reproduced, stored in a retrieval system or transmitted in any form or by any means – electronic, mechanical, photocopying, recording, or any other – except for brief quotations in printed reviews, without the prior written permission of the publisher.

Editor: Rhonda Crowder

Cover and Interior Design: Wayne Dailey

ISBN: 978-0-9835218-2-2

All Scripture quotations are taken from the King James Version of the Holy Bible

Library of Congress Control Number: 2019909110

Printed in the United States of America

Contact: byrondemery.com

INTRODUCTION

Imagine having to muster the courage to swallow a pill you knew would be painful and would change your life in a drastic way. Imagine after swallowing this pill, the walls of your life closing in and the pressure mounting. Imagine seemingly lacking the sustainable strength to go forward but still having to care for three children and an ex-spouse who depend on you deeply. Imagine, while going through this experience, GOD providing you a testimony to share with as many who will receive it. The person I am describing is me and my real life wilderness experience is outlined in this book.

My name is Byron Demery. At forty-one years old, I have been married, am the proud father of three children and have worked in government for most of my career. To date in my life, I haven't accomplished anything famous or newsworthy. On the surface, I've done nothing that would justify me writing a book about it. The only incredible thing I have managed to do is survive a growing process and experience over twenty-four months that inspired me to write this book.

This experience began with an unfortunate event, a failure. I failed as a husband in my marriage. Yes, I admit this. Like others, I entered into a marriage without fully understanding my role as a "Christian Man" in the relationship. My former spouse also made mistakes. We both did.

As a couple, our initial mistake was not seeking proper counseling prior to entering into such a sacred commitment. It's unfortunate that the divorce rate is as high as it is, even among Christians. I swallowed the pill of dissolving my marriage, not knowing where life would take me. I truly entered the wilderness and had so many unanswered questions about my future.

However, this wilderness and uncertainty is what GOD used to build my faith and reliance on HIM. Times were dark but necessary for my personal growth and spiritual development. Who is JEHOVAH GOD, our Heavenly Father, and do you truly know HIM? If asked this question before my experience, my reply would have been both "yes" and "no." Yes, I grew up in church, and was baptized by the age of ten. From a youth up until my late thirties, I had a good understanding of GOD but I did not truly know HIM for myself.

That all changed within my wilderness experience.

Before my experience, I perceived myself as being a respectable guy. I came from a good family. I held a Master's degree, gainful employment and took care of my family. I had ambition, suitable maturity and was perceived as a "good catch." My then wife would often receive compliments about me.

However, as the years went by, she became less impressed.

For the last seven years of our marriage, the relationship was a constant struggle. At times, as a man and husband, I felt inadequate.

Having dated since college, my then wife and I finally reached a point where we both decided to end our marital relationship. I am not sure she would have decided to go through with it if I had not advocated to do so. She may have been content with the status quo of us living together unhappily and raising three children.

However, the growing resentment we had towards each other, wrapped inside our constant arguing, started to affect our children. The marriage counseling we attended did not help resolve matters and I knew in my heart something had to change.

I followed my heart, took a leap of faith and jumped. This jump started me down a path. At times, this path was slow, painful, frustrating and worrisome. It could have left me bitter and unappreciative. However, because of my experience, the spiritual fruits of faith, longsuffering, peace, temperance, kindness and love took root. For this growth and process, I am forever thankful and reminded daily of how blessed I truly am.

Most importantly, through my experience, I got a chance to witness and confirm for myself the true nature of GOD. As a child growing up in church, I often heard people giving testimonies of who GOD was and what HE meant in their lives. However, as HIS child, it's nothing like knowing HIM individually! In learning HIM for myself, I began to mature in the ways of the Spirit and to digest meat instead of drinking milk.

In essence, I became more full of HIM. Admittedly this fullness and maturity only came as a byproduct of time, pain, suffering, doubt and a lot of uncertainty. Many times throughout my experience, I constantly asked myself the questions of when, why and how?

By the grace of GOD, I am here today to testify of HIS goodness. This is the reason why I decided to write this book. I would feel extreme remorse to not profess how GOD sustained me throughout this most challenging time in my life. I felt others could truly benefit from my story, my testimony.

Along with writing this as a professing Christian, I am also writing this as a forty-one year old natural man who has dealt with challenges both in my personal and professional life. I have encountered both failure and success. I know the feeling and pressure of being a husband, father and provider all at the same time.

As men, I believe we often try to walk this tightrope and juggle all three of these roles and relationships simultaneously without expectation of failing or falling. At times, the pressure can seem too much and suffocating. As a man, you can sometimes feel inept. I can relate to this feeling.

Even though I am attempting to impact lives through this book, I currently do not hold the title of a minister or a pastoral leader. An inside part of me truly feels that, one day, I will be called to hold an office within church. However, currently I am authoring this book only as an evolved, professing Christian Man. One who still makes mistakes and falls short but is dedicated to continue evolving to be all that GOD, our Heavenly Father, willed me to be!

This book is not a prosperity message nor is it a pity party about my pain. It is divided into months, not chapters, to chronicle the details of my life over a two-year period. A time when I was tried the most yet able to persevere and endure. All the months combined equate to one huge chapter, one I call my *wilderness experience.*

This place will always be near and dear to me because I got to know GOD more intimately.

In closing this introduction, I want to say there are no good or bad people in this story. I am not the hero or perfect character. I am just one who learned a lot along the way. If you are looking for some encouragement in order to gain perseverance in the midst of trials, this book offers it. If you are looking for the overall message of faith and love, this book offers it. If you are looking for an example of how someone can evolve and change despite tough times, this book offers it. If you are looking for a testimony on how GOD can sustain you during these times, this book offers that as well.

Perhaps the greatest gift someone can give is to encourage others by sharing their own testimony. I gratefully and unselfishly offer you this gift inside the pages of this book. Please sit back and graciously enjoy this roller coaster ride of ups and downs, twists and turns and joys and pain. I pray it will help you along the way, wherever you are on your current journey in life. May it challenge you to evolve into the Christian you aspire to be.

03.2016

month 1

This story begins in March of 2016, the first month of my wilderness experience. It is the moment I made a wholehearted decision about one main concern in my life: my marriage. I remember visiting Las Vegas with my father and brother for a couple days during the beginning of the NCAA Men's College Basketball Tournament otherwise known as March Madness. It was an enjoyable time to just relax, watch television and see if any major upsets happened. With no itinerary attached, I had the pleasure of rooming with my father.

Over the years the relationship between my father and I had evolved. Growing up, he was the less vocal parent. He usually resorted to my mother being the one who would talk to and discipline us children when needed. However, as I grew older and began having children of my own, him and I talked more. I enjoyed his perspective on things, not only as my father but as an older, more experienced Christian man.

"How are things going on the job, at home?" he asked.

"Status quo. No new complaints but no exciting news either," I replied.

At the time, I had been waiting on some changes to happen in my life that seemed to be delayed for some reason. However, I began to realize GOD was waiting on me to finish something I should have resolved some years ago. Until, I took action to end my marriage, HE would not begin to move in other areas of my life. It was a very challenging, scary truth to accept.

"Pop, I realize that my marriage has to end," I sadly but truthfully expressed.

"Son, you have battled with this issue for some time now. You took steps to do this before, but decided not to follow through with it. Are you sure about this? I agree that this may be best for your wife and you," he answered.

My father knew of some of the issues my marriage faced and doubted things would improve in order for the relationship between my wife and I to flow as a healthy marriage should. I needed those couple days in Las Vegas to refocus my thoughts and prepare myself to have a real heart to heart talk with my wife upon returning home. We had started having these talks over the previous couple of months, but needed to begin seriously have them.

There were a lot of things to be leery of. I knew divorce could be a potential wealth killer and that it made good common and biblical sense for two to labor towards common goals instead of one. Most importantly, as a child, I never had to deal with the issue of divorce, so how it could impact my children lived in the front of my mind.

I was not an advocate of divorce. I still believed marriage could be a beautiful experience, between the right two people, at the right time. However, I had to face reality. I found myself in a relationship with ineffective communication, intimacy at a low point and trust hard to come by. She and I both were truly unhappy with each other. She did not truly regard me as her husband and I did not cherish her as my wife. Neither of us seemed willing to give more to heal the relationship due to the hurt and disappointment of the past. Marriage counseling had not worked and we both grew tired of going through the motions. Despite having three young children to consider, something had to give.

04.2016

month 2

Upon returning from Las Vegas, I did exactly what I said I would. I had a heavy conversation with my wife and brought up the idea of divorce. It happened on a Sunday morning in the kitchen after breakfast. She was in a relatively peaceful mood and the kids were off somewhere running around the house.

"I know we have casually mentioned this before, do you still want a divorce?" I delicately asked while washing the dishes.

"Yes," she calmly replied. "I am tired of feeling neglected in this relationship and feeling like you don't care about what I need. I'm ready."

In my mind, I couldn't believe we were actually having this conversation. Surprisingly, it did not lead to any arguing or finger-pointing as she supported ending the marriage. During the conversation, we both reflected on what we promised each other three years prior during the birth of our third child. We had agreed to give our marriage another try for the sake of our children. However, if unhappiness continued, we would not stay together just for the kids. We did not want to raise them in an environment where we would continue to argue. That was not the picture of marriage we wanted them to see. One of constant struggle, confusion and a seeming lack of love.

"So," I continued, "Are you going to hire an attorney or do I need to?"

To my financial benefit, she replied, "Yes, I will hire an attorney."

From there, things moved quickly. So fast, I knew GOD was in the midst of this decision. In recognizing from past experiences, when GOD is ready to move, HE moves quickly. Within a blink of an eye, situations could change. In fact, by April 11th, I already had draft dissolution documents sent to me for review. We had discussed the financial issues needing to be addressed. And, for the most part, we easily agreed on everything except who would stay in the house and who needed to move.

We did not want to sell the house because the children were comfortable there and the two oldest enjoyed attending the local elementary school, just a short walk away. I argued since the house was solely deeded to me and the mortgage was my liability, I should be the one to stay. She thought otherwise as we went back and forth about this for a couple weeks. Over this time, the facial expressions and tone of voice we exchanged over this issue became unpleasant.

Finally, because I wanted out of the marriage and to ease tension in the house, I consented. I agreed to allow her to continue living in the house with the kids. In return, she would be responsible for making the monthly mortgage payment. After this last issue was settled, I received the final separation agreement.

Within a month, the terms of the dissolution were agreed upon with minimal conflict. I had heard horror stories about couples going through divorce and how unpleasant, stressful and expensive it could turn out. Thank GOD we were able to avoid hostility, proving HE was in the midst of our decision.

05.2016

month 3

On an early afternoon at the beginning of the month, the time came for my wife and I to meet at her attorney's office and sign all the documents for the dissolution of marriage filing. Things were going so smoothly we rode to the appointment together. Upon walking in, I met her attorney, a slender, middle-aged Caucasian lady with red orange hair. She extended her hand to shake mine.

"I have heard good things about you," she said, as I extended my hand.

"Thank you," I said politely. I appreciated her warm welcome.

The signing of documents took less than an hour. During that time, everything seemed so quiet and still. The three of us sat in a mid-size conference room and you could have heard a pin drop. During the signing, I did not feel any uneasiness in my spirit at all. Once completed, the attorney handed me my copies.

"I'll be filing the petition tomorrow," she said.

As we exited the attorney's office, I remember feeling okay with everything. However, my wife remained quiet and her face did not reveal much.

"Are you okay?" I asked.

"Yes," she calmly responded. "You?"

Just as calm, I said, "Yes."

After I dropped her off at work, I remember feeling a huge weight being lifted. I was in disbelief that dissolution papers were being filed to end my marriage only forty-five days after returning from Las Vegas. I could not believe GOD was allowing this. It seemed surreal in a lot of ways. A lot of thoughts and feelings crossed my mind.

Later in the month, our family took a vacation on a four-day, three-night Disney Cruise that had been planned for over a year. An older female friend traveled with us and my wife and I were determined to have a good time despite the recent turn of events. Our children still didn't know and, for the time being, we wanted to act normal. However, I had a hunch our female friend knew. In knowing my wife and I for years, she probably thought we were doing the best thing too.

The Disney Cruise was expensive but an experience we really enjoyed knowing substantial changes were on the horizon. Along with the pending dissolution, my wife planned to have major surgery in late June and would be unable to physically be active with the kids for some weeks while recovering. In addition, I had to find a place to live. My wife had been asking me to move out since March. However, I refused to go anywhere until I knew the dissolution would go forward. With the petition now filed, and expenses from the attorney incurred, she really turned up the heat on this issue.

The idea of finding somewhere else to live was hard for me to grasp. Even though I had consented to move, it felt like I was being forced out of my house. I had not rented in several years and was not fond of my last experience. Back in 2012, the last time we separated, I moved out and into an apartment. The space was small and the adjustment hard. I had this claustrophobic feeling while staying there. At the time, I only had two children, so an apartment worked. However, now with three kids, I had to find a house with enough bedrooms and space to accommodate all of us.

I remembered talking, back in March, to a work colleague of mine. Despite being employed in a different department, we had known each other since I started my tenure with the organization and maintained a good rapport. I went to his office about a work-related matter and we happened to strike up a conversation. He mentioned a house he was trying to sell due to moving into another residence. I told him I might be interested in possibly renting it. By April, this interest had fully grown and I politely asked him to show me the residence. We drove there one day on lunch and I really liked the house. It was in a good neighborhood and had plenty of space, with a nice backyard and central air.

I explained my personal situation and asked if he would be willing to rent the property to me with a June move in date. This timeline worked for him since he still had to remove some debris out of the house and get a hole in the garage roof repaired. He told me "yes" but stated he needed to run the decision by his wife. I understood and told him to get back with me as soon as possible. I got excited and thought to myself, "Hey, I didn't even have to look for a house. I miraculously happened to stumble upon one while striking up a conversation at work." It felt too good to be true.

Still in May, the issue of having a place to live remained unresolved. My work colleague had politely told me "no." His wife did not think renting the house to me was a clever idea. I quickly got over the unfortunate news and thought to myself, "There must be another house out there for me." While I remained calm about my living situation, my wife grew more anxious. Disappointed about the news on my work colleague's house, once again she asked where I planned to live.

"You told me you were finding a place to live," she disappointedly expressed.

"I've started looking. Now that the dissolution papers are filed and the cruise is over, I can devout more time to the issue," I responded.

"Do you need me to help you find a place?" she asked.

"No, I can take care of it myself," I calmly responded.

I begin checking local newspaper listings and online resources. One of the biggest changes I noticed was how much people advertised rental properties online for free as opposed to paying for an ad in the newspaper. Someone recommended I try Craigslist.

I did and within a week found a house located on the same street where my work colleague owned the other house. Remembering the street and its quietness, I contacted the person listed and expressed my interest. A couple of days from there, I was sent a rental application to complete. Another possibility surfaced.

06.2016

month 4

With my wife's surgery set for the 24th, June was a critical month. The physician in charge had been my wife's OBGYN since giving birth to our second child. She trusted him wholeheartedly which gave her the courage to go through with the procedure.

In addition to the surgery, the final dissolution court date was scheduled for late July. Aware of the pressing need to finalize my living arrangement, I submitted my rental application for the house listed on Craigslist and waited for a response. One of the property owners did have one question. On the application, I noted my current address as a house I owned. She questioned why I expressed an interest in renting her property since I already owned? I explained my marital situation and she understood.

She then approved my application and scheduled an appointment to show the house.

I took my two sons with me to see the property. The owners, an older married couple, were already inside when I pulled up to a white house with a narrowly paved driveway. Upon walking in, the interior impressed me. The house seemed bigger than it appeared from the outside and had nice decor. To the right was an upgraded kitchen with remodeled cabinets and a polished wood floor. To the left, there was a carpeted recreation room for the kids. Throughout the house there was also four carpeted bedrooms and two bathrooms, both with showers. The house also included a new furnace, central air and a built in area off the side of the kitchen to fit a washer and dryer. Outside, the single car garage was suitable for my vehicle and the backyard large enough for the kids to run around.

The property owners seemed friendly. We exchanged conversation on our respective backgrounds.

"So how long have you lived in the area?" they asked, almost simultaneously.

"All my life. I am the last of my immediate family here. Everyone else has moved away," I responded.

"Where did they relocate?" asked the female property owner.

"My sister lives in Cincinnati. My brother is in Northern Virginia and my parents are in Louisville, Kentucky," I replied.

"Louisville, I used to live there and know the area very well," she responded.

"I understand you work for the City?" the male property owner continued.

"Yes, I have for the past eleven years," I answered.

"I retired from the City's Fire Department after thirty years of service," he replied.

Based on our conversation, there was common ground and a connection made. I even learned both owners were previously divorced before remarrying each other. Upon leaving the house, I confirmed my interest in living there and wanted to bring my daughter back next weekend before making a final decision. At that time, I would sign a lease to begin living there in July.

Next weekend my daughter accompanied me to the house for the follow up visit to see if she would like the new living arrangement. On the way, we had an emotional talk. She and my oldest son had come to understand what was going on with their mother and I and the situation did not seem to distress them too much. Fortunately, all this was happening during the summer and did not serve as an immediate distraction during the school year. Being older, my daughter was more concerned and vocal about the matter.

"Dad, I know a lot of people especially kids think divorce is bad. We don't understand why parents who love each other just can't work things out," she said.

"I understand how you feel and want you to know the issues between your mother and I have nothing to do with you or your brothers," I told her.

"Well, I know both of you are tired of arguing with each other. Maybe it's the best thing," she responded.

"We would not be doing it if we did not think it was best. Regardless, our love for you three children will never change. We love all of you very much and are blessed to be your parents," I reassured her.

After walking through the house, the new living arrangement met my daughter's approval. She particularly liked the size of the bedrooms and the upstairs bathroom with shower. By the grace of GOD, I signed my lease with the targeted move in date of July 10th. This was a huge burden that had been lifted! I could inform my wife that I had secured a place to live. GOD was good!

My high from the previous week carried over into a wedding on June 18th. A childhood friend of mine and my wife's sister got married. The two of them had known each other for some years and met for the first time at my parents' old house. In a way, I felt both responsible and credited for their union. It seemed ironic that I was going to congratulate these two on their special day, while in the process of ending my marriage. I thought to myself that's just the way life goes sometimes.

My wife and daughter were in the ceremony, so we had to be on time. I remember dropping them off at the door to find parking and walking into the church. I found a seat on the rear left side of the sanctuary minutes before the wedding began. The ceremony was short but sweet. My daughter was so moved by it she cried tears of happiness. I remember the minister reciting the vows with the bride and groom and listening to what both of them committed to, before GOD, with all of us as witnesses. As I listened, I said to myself, "If I ever again stand before GOD and recited vows, I'm keeping them."

After the ceremony and required photos, we drove a short distance to the reception. Being hungry I hoped the food would be tasty. They held the party at a banquet center with noticeable white pillars at the main entrance. The bright ceiling lights lit the party room very well, highlighting a spacious, polished wood dance floor with a disco ball. White cloths with matching colored plates, light grey napkins and black silverware covered the tables.

Overall, I really enjoyed myself and talked with people I had not seen in years! The food met my expectations and seeing my children and their cousins dancing truly brought me joy. Despite the pleasant time, there were some people present who felt a certain way about the dissolution of my marriage. I received an awkward look from my wife's aunt. Obviously, she knew about the pending situation. I let that negativity roll right off me. I knew we were making the right decision to end the marriage despite the thoughts and opinions of others.

As the reception continued, our decision confirmed itself. For most of the celebration, my wife sat at the head table with the wedding party. As the reception started winding down, we decided to try and dance to a slow song. Still being her husband, it felt only right to ask my wife to dance.

Looking over at her, I extended the invitation, "Would you like to dance?"

She seemed surprised I asked but replied, "Yes."

As we drew closer on the dance floor and touched hands, something did not feel right. I sensed some hesitancy from both of us. Physically, she looked fine. She wore a black dress with silver trim that complemented her nicely. Her hair was done and makeup up to par. She looked delightful. Outwardly, I had a fresh haircut and wore a grey blazer with black dress pants which complemented her attire. However, as we danced and looked at each other, we smirked. I said to myself, "What are we doing?" and imagined her saying the same. The song playing was no indication of our marital relationship. The emotional connection we once shared had evaporated.

I graciously asked her, "You want to stop?"

She calmly replied, "Yes."

We let go of each other's hand and slowly walked away parting before the song ended. Our exit from the dance floor was a bittersweet ending to a wonderful day. It confirmed our marriage had run its course and was approaching the end.

The following week, the morning of the surgery, we had to be at the hospital early. I made sure to take a book to read, knowing I'd have a long wait time during her procedure. My in-laws and some close friends joined to see my wife off during the preparation, until they put her under. As they wheeled her back to the operating room, I just remember thinking how badly she needed the procedure. Truthfully, we both needed it. Due to the pending dissolution, I needed her to be in better health to properly care for the children upon recovery.

The surgery waiting room was spacious and comfortable. There were plenty of sitting areas, televisions and power outlets for charging electronics. Hot coffee with a Subway and a cafeteria nearby helped too. I needed all these amenities as the surgery went longer than expected. What was anticipated to be done in three hours went past four. I began to get a little nervous after being relatively calm at the beginning. When the doctor came out, he sat my mother-in-law and myself down and went through the details.

He showed us some pictures and explained the "before" and "after" of the operation. We tried to understand what he displayed and asked questions as to why the surgery went so long.

"We encountered more internal bleeding than anticipated, which made operating more difficult," he said.

After a couple days, the hospital released my wife. On the way home, I drove straight to the pharmacy to get her pain medication. She experienced a lot of pain as a result of the procedure and, without that medication, would not have survived. After pulling into the driveway, I gently helped her out of the car and slowly up the steps into the family room where a bed was set up for her. With a bathroom nearby and a television in front of her, she could access all she needed. I knew it would be a long recovery process, but we had to get through it. Despite our marriage ending, we still needed each other.

07.2016

month 5

Only out of surgery for a week, my wife still experienced a lot of pain. However, she started getting around better and making progress in routine activities. Many visitors came by to see her so the house had not been quiet. Everyday, people stopped by, called and prepared meals to show their support. While we appreciated all their efforts, she needed to get some rest. I decided to take the kids to my parents' house in Kentucky for the Fourth of July weekend.

I did not feel comfortable going at first. Some family and close friends said they would make sure my wife had food to eat and would come by and check on her. She and I talked about it and weighed the dependability of those who said they would help. Two people for sure we knew would not let us down, so she gave her consent and told me to take the kids out of town. The house would be quiet and she could relax and rest well for three days.

The kids and I left that Friday and returned the following Monday. We had a great time with my parents and my wife was in better spirits upon our return. She welcomed the children home with the warmest smile when they rushed through the door. I knew she rested while we were gone and it showed. She was more talkative and her overall mood was better.

On the horizon, the final dissolution hearing was scheduled for the end of the month. Before then, I had to move my belongings into the new house. I planned to move in on the day my lease started. My landlords were gracious enough to sell me three beds and two window air conditioning units on credit. With enough beds and my U-Haul truck rented, I was ready. To keep my children from being a distraction that day, my wife and her friend took them somewhere that morning. She did not need to be present since we had already decided what I would take from the main house.

I went to pick up the moving truck at 10 a.m. and backed it into the driveway. I hoped none of my neighbors noticed me. Despite knowing I was making the right decision, I still felt embarrassed. Nobody wants to admit to their neighbors that their marriage is not working, that they are moving out and getting a divorce. I did not know how that would be perceived. Would I be looked upon as a bad "man" or "father?" I just did not feel like fielding any questions.

One of my helpers arrived and we began moving things into the truck swiftly. We talked about random things which seemed to make the furniture less burdensome. For some reason, I had plenty of energy. It's not that I slept so well the previous night, I just knew this day had arrived. It felt awkward but refreshing at the same time. The third mover came around 11:30 a.m. and helped us finish loading the truck. Everything fit into one load and we were off to my new residence.

Upon backing the moving truck into the driveway of the new house, I gave the fellas a quick tour of the place and we took a short break. By the time 4 p.m. rolled around, we were finished. I graciously thanked them for their tremendous help and then called my wife. She and the kids had already returned to the main house. I took the moving truck back and headed that way. After arriving at the house and talking with her for a while, I asked if I could stay for a couple more nights while I got things better situated for the kids at my new residence. Plus, I figured she could use my assistance since she was still recovering from surgery.

To my surprise, she replied, "No."

I felt upset to say the least but saw no reason to argue. I grabbed what I needed and tried not to forget anything. Within thirty minutes, the kids and I were on our way. The separation was real now and I had to accept it.

A few days later, after work, I called my wife and asked to stop by the main house to gather a couple more things. She agreed to let me come by. When I pulled up and tried to get into the house, my key didn't work. *She had changed the locks!* A wave of rejection hit me and I had to gather myself to avoid shedding the tear in my eye. The hurt ensued as I couldn't believe she would have this done after only two days of me moving out. But what was done was done, and I had to get over it and move on.

From that point, the final dissolution hearing couldn't come quick enough. My wife continued recovering, but was not at full strength going into the court date. She thought about requesting to delay the dissolution hearing due to her physical condition. Her attorney advised against it because this would have been the second time the hearing was rescheduled. If we didn't finalize the dissolution within a certain time period, the case would have to be refiled as a divorce. This would cost more time and money, which neither one of us wanted.

On the morning of the 28th, I remember feeling at peace. I had secured a place to live and came prepared to answer any questions the judge might ask. I went to the hearing alone, but I wasn't there by myself. GOD was with me. I knew HE was with me. I felt at ease.

My wife looked nice and personable that morning as she sat outside the courtroom with her attorney. We waited for about an hour and a half before our case was called. When we walked up to the judge's bench, my wife and I vowed to tell the truth under oath.

The judge, an elderly Caucasian lady, wore her glasses on the tip of her nose. Looking down from the bench, she took a good, intimidating glance at both of us as she reviewed the paperwork in front of her. She asked my wife three to four questions and then had a few for me. Her main concern was our children and their care.

"Ma'am, I understand you are the mother of the three children involved?" the judge asked.

My wife replied, "Yes, I am."

"Are you working, Ma'am?" the judge asked.

"Yes, I work at a local non-profit," she answered.

"I understand the children will be primarily residing with you. Are there any other concerns with their care or this case I should be made aware of?" the judge asked.

My wife replied, "No, your Honor."

The judge then turned her attention to me.

"Sir, are you the father of the three children involved?" she asked.

"Yes, Ma'am, I am" I replied.

"Sir, it says here you work for the City. How long have you been employed there?" she asked.

"I have been employed there for eleven years," I answered.

"Sir, have you secured a place to live?" the judge asked.

"Yes, I have your Honor," I answered.

Within 10 minutes, she granted the dissolution and the hearing ended. I walked out of the courtroom, said goodbye to my wife and thanked her attorney for her help in the process. Her attorney wished me the best of luck and I knew she believed I was a decent guy who tried to make the process as painless as possible.

I had walked the walk and accomplished what I set out to do in five short months. It felt so monumental! Not to glamorize the dissolution, but I knew that a major step had been taken. It was unimaginable to believe that this was even possible, especially with three young children. However, it happened in such a brief period of time and in such a peaceful way. I knew GOD was with me!

Within the month of July my marriage ended. My wife was now solely the mother of my children and I was ready to begin a new chapter in my life, a chapter that left a lot of things uncertain. However, a chapter I had to turn the page and begin.

08.2016

month 6

The first month having to honor all the financial obligations of the dissolution rolled in with the furiousness of a lion's roar. I had to pay a full month of rent for my new residence and child support. With all that going on, I remained in decent spirits. We celebrated my oldest son's sixth birthday earlier in the montah and it reminded me that I was still blessed in so many ways. To assist me financially, my parents graciously offered to help me with rent for the month and I gratefully accepted.

One day at work, while walking down the hallway returning from lunch, I received a surprise phone call from the mother of my children. The conversation was short and ended on a sour note.

"Hello," I said.

"Hey, we need to talk. It's important," she replied.

"Go ahead. I'm listening."

"I can't afford to pay childcare anymore," she stated.

"Why not? What's going on?" I answered.

"The additional expense of leasing a new car will eat up a lot of my budget. You're going to have to start paying childcare for all the kids going forward," she explained.

Previously, she drove a vehicle I leased, which had been turned into the dealer based on the terms of the dissolution. Now, with a new lease under her name, she felt the financial pinch. Childcare was the one thing we did not clearly negotiate terms on in our dissolution. Lesson learned, I should have included this expense. When I brought up this subject before, noting it was not in the dissolution agreement, she stated verbally that it was not a big deal and it would continue to be paid the same way. I paid for before and after school care for the two oldest children and she paid for the youngest child's daycare.

In trying to remain calm, I replied, "Hey, we need to talk more about this, I can't afford to pay more childcare. I am not agreeing to do this. Please reconsider what you are asking me to do. I can't afford it," I argued.

"Well, sorry you need to figure it out," she replied.

As I began to say something else, she ended the conversation and hung up the phone. I tried to call her back and she would not pick up. I was aggravated but did not see the point of continuing trying to contact her. In one short phone conversation my finances had shifted even more!

After some days, we had a chance to talk and I again emphasized that I could not afford this new expense. She defended her position and stated she could not either. She agreed to pay the expense for the rest of the month to give me a brief time to make the adjustment. After that, the responsibility would be mine. In my mind, I asked myself, "How can I afford this? I can't!"

The money I thought would be saved by no longer making monthly car payments on the turned in lease was being redirected to more childcare expenses. With no guarantee of how long my parents could assist me with rent on the new house, next month my cash flow would go further in the red. I already struggled paying for everything.

I asked the question, "Where is GOD? LORD where are YOU?" I had this impression in my mind that GOD knew I would need additional money due to the dissolution and the additional expense it would cost me. I had been desiring another job for some time and thought for sure HE would provide now! After all, I did what HE asked me to do. I turned the corner and went through with the dissolution. Surely, HE would hear my prayers and answer. In my mind, I had done everything I was supposed to do to receive a breakthrough.

However, I saw no breakthrough in sight. I had applied for a Budget Manager position with a local college the previous month, trying to secure better pay. When looking at the position description, I met all the qualifications and thought for sure my application would be viewed favorably. On August 22nd, I received an email from the human resources department of the college stating the interview process for the position had been completed. Here, I took the time to beat the deadline and apply for a position I thought was a good fit and I did not even get selected for an interview.

I felt dejected and devalued.

The funny and blessed thing is, GOD always has a way of reminding you HE is near even though you do not feel HIM! Not only was my personal life going through twists and turns, my work life had added pressure as well. At the end of August, there was a big meeting scheduled that had my immediate supervisor overly anxious and even the Director of my department concerned. It was an annual committee meeting I had previously attended and presented at. However, this year the committee had a new chairperson. The word going around was the new chair was tough, asked a lot of questions and scrutinized everything. Heading into the meeting, none of my supervisors or I expected business as usual.

The meeting was scheduled for an early afternoon time on the last Thursday of the month. The day prior, I had the pleasure of meeting the new chairperson when I dropped off some information for her review. She was courteous in meeting me for the first time, but not overly polite. I left the information with her along with my business card and regards until the following day.

The morning of the 25th, I remember fervently praying to the LORD. In my prayers, I asked HIM to be in the meeting with me. I prayed for HIM to have HIS WAY in the meeting. As we began walking to the meeting that afternoon, I felt a little anxious but prepared. My guns were fully loaded to answer any questions that could arise.

As the meeting was about to begin, the chairperson walked into the conference room and introduced herself. She extended a professional greeting to everyone and specifically requested that I sit next to her. My immediate supervisor and Director were a little puzzled by her request but gave the go-ahead for me to sit there. The meeting got off to a rocky start and I was sure the new chairperson would ask more questions just to assert her position. Sitting next to her, I noticed she had written notes and question marks on the information I previously provided her.

However, as the meeting went on, she never asked the questions I thought she would. She settled down, the meeting sped up and before you knew it all business had been concluded in a record time of twenty-eight minutes! As the meeting adjourned, my immediate supervisor appeared shocked at the outcome and went on to openly commend me in front of the committee. My

Director was in such a good mood and so light on her feet after leaving the meeting she treated herself and I to an afternoon desert and iced tea on the way back to the office. I was floating on cloud nine and, amazingly, none of this was of my own doing.

I did not have to answer a slew of questions or "work" to get the result I hoped for. THE LORD HAD HIS WAY in that meeting! I stood out without having to try and HE showed out on my behalf. Never would I have imagined a situation that appeared so problematic, so worrisome would turn out the way it did. GOD gave me exceedingly above what I had asked and hoped for! The favorable, short meeting was HIS WAY of showing HE stills answers prayer and was with me. I desperately needed this confirmation and victory at this time in my experience.

09.2016

month 7

Despite my victory at the end of August, my mind was back on pins and needles in September. In trying to keep my mind at ease, I would reflect on *Philippians 4:6-8* to remind myself not to be anxious over anything but with prayer and supplication to make my request known unto GOD. I also tried to reflect on all the positive things in my life and how GOD had been there for me. I reminded myself that HE would not bring me this far to leave me. However, guarding my heart and mind was a tough task as things got more difficult.

The mother of my children had returned to work, which was financially good. The negative was that she was really fatigued. She was constantly tired and could not keep the children overnight and still go to work the next day. As a result, the children ended up staying with me during the work week and spent the weekends with her. However, even on the weekends, I found myself spending a lot of time at the main house helping her with the kids. This was not what I imagined happening. The whole point of the dissolution was for us to separate. Instead we saw each other about every day and there was no real separation at all. People questioned what was going on and why the situation was evolving into what it was.

Personally, I had a two-way struggle going on. I struggled being around the mother of my children without feeling thoughts of resentment and anger. The dissolution was just finalized back in July and I still had anger inside me towards her. It was hard for me to see her as often as I did and not feel a certain way. Her emotions were also all over the place most of the time which made communication that much more difficult. Due to this difficulty, we found it easier to text message each other instead of having verbal conversations.

Due to my tight financial situation, I considered applying for a part time job or possibly driving for Uber. However, due to family obligations, my schedule was mostly spoken for. My parents decided once again to help me with rent. Due to their generosity, I was able to add cable and internet to the new house and purchase an inexpensive Hisense Smart television and stand. After purchasing these essential items, I felt a sense of accomplishment. The new house was finally looking like a place where my children could enjoy similar comforts as the main one. Despite the struggle, I was making things work as best I could.

The mother of my children was in a comparable financial situation. She had not paid the mortgage on the main house for August, and since this was her biggest expense, it was the one she struggled to pay the most. Instead of questioning her finances and spending, I tried to be proactive and reach out to the bank to see what could be worked out. I disclosed my financial information and the terms of the dissolution to see if some relief could be granted.

Unfortunately, after reviewing my request, the bank denied any relief based on the fact that I did not currently reside in the house. The news was disappointing, but I said to myself that things would somehow work out. The mortgage payment on the main house for August was made late September. I knew the mother of my children's ability to pay the mortgage would continually be an uphill battle. This added additional stress to our situation.

The dissolution was beginning to stretch her and me both emotionally and financially. Even though things for us appeared to be getting worse before getting better, I still did not have any regrets on dissolving the marriage. I knew it was the right decision for us. I was still asking the questions of what, when, why and how of GOD? However, I had to keep it together because of the three young children. They needed my care, love, guidance and support now more than ever. I was determined to not let them down because they deserved better. I had to be strong.

In trying to develop some peace, I surrounded myself with necessary support. In the mornings, I typically started my day with quiet time and prayer. On the way to work, I listened to the Erica Campbell Morning Show to surround myself with the presence of GOD through song. In remembering *Romans 10:17*, I positioned myself to hear the WORD OF GOD more to strengthen my FAITH.

My favorite pastime was listening to Charles Stanley. I would usually be home alone on Sunday mornings, the perfect time to hear his message. The quietness ushered in a priceless connection. I remember particularly listening to Pastor Stanley on the last Sunday of the month as he spoke on the title message of *Advancing Your Faith*. That message stuck with me and I knew GOD spoke to me through him.

At this point, I did not know how long my wilderness experience would last or how things would turn out. However, I knew my FAITH would be tested to strengthen and grow like never before.

KEY VERSES

As it is written,

"Be careful for nothing; but in every thing by prayer and supplication with thanksgiving let your requests be made known unto God. And the peace of God, which passeth all understanding, shall keep your hearts and minds through Christ Jesus. Finally, brethren, whatsoever things are true, whatsoever things are honest, whatsoever things are just, whatsoever things are pure, whatsoever things are lovely, whatsoever things are of good report; if there be any virtue, and if there be any praise, think on these things."
Philippians 4:6-8

"So then faith cometh by hearing, and hearing by the word of God."
Romans 10:17

10.2016

month 8

With October underway, my children were now comfortable spending time at both houses and seemed to be focused in school. As a fourth grader, my daughter maintained a heavy workload and amazed me with all the things she was learning. She usually had homework every night. After dinner, I would review it and help her with any questions. Feeling my burden, the mother of my children began to keep the kids at least once during the work week, which I appreciated. On those nights, I would usually treat myself to a sit down dinner with a beer to relax. If I felt extra adventurous, I would watch a movie when I got home.

To my vital benefit, my parents once again helped me with rent at the new house. Over the years, I grew to appreciate them more and more. Their love for me remained unconditional and their support unwavering. A lot of my high school classmates had lost either one or both their parents. I felt blessed and fortunate to have mine alive and in my life.

Despite the love, encouragement and support from others, the questions of what, when, why and how were still ever present in my mind. I wish I could say some peace had developed mentally for me, but I remained anxious about a lot of things. I did not know what the future held. Financially, due to my parents helping me with rent, I was still able to pay most of my bills with the exception of some credit cards that fell further behind. The mother of my children still struggled with paying the mortgage on the main house with payments constantly made thirty days late. Between the credit card bills I could not afford to pay and the late mortgage payments, my personal credit took an immense hit.

It seemed the choices I had made were not paying off and were in vain. However, I still believed dissolving my marriage was the right thing to do. I also still knew GOD was with me. Those two constants stayed on my mind. However, I did not know what GOD was up to and what HE was doing. I worried and thought about things too much. I was in the wilderness and my thoughts were unsure.

I was seemingly lost.

When going through a wilderness experience, it's hard to not worry. It's only naturally human to react that way. In studying the Old Testament, I began to understand why Moses was needed to lead the Israelites out of Egypt. If they were to travel through the wilderness alone without a leader, they would have been lost without any sense of direction. They did not know where they were going and neither did Moses. However, Moses had GOD, who provided needed direction to him that was then given to the people, even if they at times rejected it. I did not have Moses, but I had the WORD OF GOD as my guide. I had to learn to embrace HIS WORD in a new way and not reject it. HIS WORD had to take root and become firm in my heart. In remembering *Romans 10:9-10*, my heart had to believe!

Being honest with myself, I was not there yet in my belief.

October ended with a special, monumental occasion happening. On the last weekend of the month, my baby sister got married! The weekend seemed surreal, especially for my parents. Both of them had doubts my sister would ever get married. My sister and her fiance asked me to be in the wedding and, of course, I said "yes." Held in a Cincinnati, Ohio wedding hall we had a blast the whole weekend. The ceremony was well planned and my sister wore the most beautiful white dress that fit her perfectly. I wore a black tuxedo with a blue vest and necktie. I looked and felt good!

Seated at the head table during the reception, it was wonderful to see everyone in attendance. A lot of members from both families came, along with a host of friends to celebrate the bride and groom. For most of my life, I typically shied away from the dance floor. However, the evening of the reception, I danced like a twenty-one year old, full of life and confidence.

For whatever reason, I danced more that night than I had in years. I am sure the alcoholic beverages played a part. My parents were ecstatic that everyone enjoyed themselves. My sister sported the brightest smile on her special day and was truly a beautiful bride! It was a great weekend, one I planned on remembering for years to come.

Sunday driving home, all we could talk about was the fun time we just had. My children, their mother and I truly enjoyed ourselves and needed my sister's wedding weekend to unwind and celebrate something positive.

The next evening, Halloween, the kids ran down the street and around the corner looking for the good candy. Their mother passed out candy, joining the neighbors in their driveway by the fire pit. A friend of the family also brought his kids over. We ate hot chili and pizza. Between my sister's memorable wedding and Halloween, I had what was needed to keep me grounded on the good things in life. I had memories and experiences of laughter, enjoyment and love. Even though my life was complicated, I still had a lot to be thankful for. My life's glass remained half full, not half empty. But being so early in my experience, I did not realize it.

KEY VERSE

As it is written,

"That if thou shalt confess with thy mouth the Lord Jesus, and shalt believe in thine heart that God hath raised him from the dead, thou shalt be saved. For with the heart man believeth unto righteousness; and with the mouth confession is made unto salvation."

Romans 10:9-10

11.2016

month 9

November represented the ninth month into my experience. A lot had happened, and I still had no idea where things were headed. I tried my best to survive mentally and get through the work week, so I could rest on the weekend. Even then, I stayed busy raking leaves and doing yard work. Financially, I cut ties with my parents supporting me and took on the obligation of paying rent at the new house. I had gotten myself into this situation and wanted to start figuring things out on my own.

In doing this, I could no longer afford to pay any of my credit card debts. While married, I struggled to pay them. Now, I simply could not afford to. My voicemail began to fill up with past due messages from creditors. Sometimes, by midday, my phone's battery would be drained from all the debt collector calls. I felt embarrassed and tried not to let anyone at my job notice how many toll free numbers called me during the day.

On a lighter note, my kids continued to enjoy spending time with me at the new house. They slept well there at night and I felt a real sense of pride in continuing to be a good father. I would cook for them, help them with homework, read them books, play games and try to do whatever else was needed so they continued to feel prioritized and loved. If I was fortunate enough to spend Friday nights with them, we would order pizza and watch movies. We watched all the historic *Star Wars* movies and the two oldest became big fans of the series.

My youngest son would sleep with me and demanded his share of the space in the bed. As much as he needed me, being scared to sleep upstairs with his brother, I needed him just as much. Little did he know, when he slept with me at night, I slept better. Many mornings I woke up to see his peaceful face lying next to me. It gave me encouragement to get up and know I had all that was needed to move forward that day.

I still had the responsibility of helping the mother of my children out on weekends. Most of the time it would be going to the grocery store with her and the kids because she could not load some of the heavier groceries into the car or carry them into the house. Also, my youngest son had yet to begin using the bathroom on his own, so I helped her juggle the diaper changes. In a lot of ways, I continued fulfilling duties as her husband. When doing this, I felt conflicted at times. But, at the end of the day, she needed help. If she needed help, why not give it? The better off she was, the better off my children were. That became my attitude about the situation.

My youngest son also turned three during the month. Due to our financial situation, we had his birthday party at Burger King. A small number of family and friends showed up and the workers there were gracious enough to let us have his party in the restaurant's play land area. It wasn't the most extravagant party, but the kids ate and were able to play. We sang *Happy Birthday* to him and passed out cupcakes. His mother and I felt bad that we hadn't done more for his birthday. But he was only three and someone so young didn't need an expensive party.

It was the first Thanksgiving since the kids were born that their mother and I were not married. However, she still wanted to come to my parents' house to celebrate the holiday. My parents left the decision up to me, so she made the trip with us. The holiday weekend was carrying on as usual with food and laughter. That's when the mother of my children received a sudden phone call that her coworker died! He recently had undergone surgery to remove some cancer in his body. While away from work on medical leave, she would usually talk with him every couple of weeks to see how his recovery was going. He would always tell her that things were looking up and seemed positive about the situation.

However, earlier that week she text messaged him and received no response. At first, she did not think anything of it and figured he may be busy. When she received the phone call about his death, it really shook her up. She cried for about an hour and reminisced on the last time she spoke with him. He was a tall, cheerful guy who always wore a big smile that could light up a room. She could not believe he was gone and she wouldn't see his big smile again. I tried to comfort her in realizing that life was short.

It made me think about what I was doing for her. A lot of people still did not understand our relationship, but I began to not care about what others thought. If I was going to be kind, why not start with her, my family? We were still on the same team, only the roles had changed. Ultimately, the goal was for the team to win, not just me. It did not cost me anything to be nicer, more supportive or less judgmental. It had taken me awhile to mature to this way of thinking, but I was finally getting there. My anger against her was beginning to subside as my heart softened.

KEY VERSE

As it is written,

"When I was a child, I spake as a child, I understood as a child, I thought as a child: but when I became a man, I put away childish things."
I Corinthians 13:11

12.2016

month 10

As the year came to an end, I wasn't in the holiday mood. With a "bah humbug" spirit, I was not looking forward to the Christmas holiday. The mother of my children and I discussed what we would try to do for the children. I had received an extra paycheck in November and, after catching up on some bills, gave her some money towards the kids' Christmas. We tried to get some of the main things they really wanted and hoped they would be content. My daughter wanted a laptop computer and, since she did not believe in Santa Claus anymore, it was easier to make her happy.

Leading up to Christmas, I didn't frequent the shopping malls or stores. The month quickly went by but it didn't feel like December because of the lack of snowfall. I was on lunch the week of Christmas, enjoying some Wendy's and received a phone call from a creditor. I let the call go to voicemail and played back the message. The creditor extended one last chance for me to work something out before taking further collection efforts on the account. Already three months behind, I did not have the money for a good faith payment on any kind of arrangement.

I was still tempted to call back but decided against it. In reality, I could not afford to pay the debt and there was nothing more to talk about. I decided I would let my credit card debt go and suffer the consequences. My personal credit was already damaged and there was no point of fighting an uphill battle I could not win. The idea of filing bankruptcy entered my mind.

The weekend of Christmas, I spent both Friday and Saturday night at the main house. This was my first time staying over since July. It felt strange, but the mother of my children needed help wrapping gifts and she seemed to enjoy my company. Christmas fell on Sunday and we were up early unwrapping gifts. With a hot cup of coffee in my hand and sleep in my eyes, I watched the magic of Christmas morning unfold. The kids gathered up all the torn wrapping paper and played with their new toys.

The most popular gift happened to be one bought the previous Christmas, a PlayStation 4 game system. This Christmas, as they opened two new games Lego Marvel Super Heroes and Disney Infinity – everything changed. *Star Wars* was on the Disney Infinity game. Being newly converted fans, my two oldest kids loved it. Also, the Lego Marvel Super Heroes game featured the Incredible Hulk, Iron Man and other characters they had come to know in movies.

We enjoyed Christmas dinner, just us as a family with no visitors. That weekend including Christmas Day was peaceful. After dinner, I prepared to leave and take the children with me so their mother could enjoy a quiet house. However, something wasn't right. She wasn't in a good place emotionally. I could tell by looking at her face.

"What's wrong?" I asked.

While trembling, she replied, "I am having an anxiety attack."

She'd had one of these attacks before and, though I'd never witnessed them, I tried to remain calm. We could not leave her in that condition so the kids and I decided to stay. She needed our love, company and comfort.

On New Year's Eve, I remember watching television and waiting for the ball to drop with my daughter. We watched Mariah Carey suffer through her pre-midnight performance. I keep asking myself, "Why is she still performing?" She didn't look enthused or prepared. As the ball dropped welcoming a New Year, I still had a lot of doubts and concerns. The year of 2016 had been one of change and challenge.

I was in the trial of my life and did not know when it would end. Despite me thinking it should have ended already, it continued and my efforts to make it end were not going anywhere. In November, I had applied for another employment opportunity that I received from a career consultant. The consultant regularly sent me available job postings and was thoughtful enough to send me this particular one on the last available day to apply. I was familiar with the organization and even knew one of the members on the Board of Directors. The old saying of, "It's not what you know but who you know" popped in my mind.

Looking at the signs, I sensed this new opportunity may have a chance. However, after speaking with my connection, he was not able to get me the job, let alone an interview. He spoke with the CEO of the organization who acknowledged receiving my application, but thought there were other stronger candidates who had applied.

I was so desperate for an opportunity, a change! However, no doors opened. It was difficult to see GOD in my situation.

01.2017

month 11

January was always a busy month for us. The first Saturday of the year we celebrated my daughter's tenth birthday. To commemorate this momentous occasion, we invited one of her classmates from school, two of her female cousins and her childhood best friend to a hotel party. It was really cold outside that weekend but felt warm and cozy inside the hotel. More like a lodge, the place had a big swimming pool, a game room and other activities for the kids to enjoy. My children's mother rented adjoining rooms with a shared patio area. The setup was great for eating, playing cards and board games.

We arrived there early afternoon with swimming on all the kids' minds. There was a small hot tub, up a short flight of steps, where the adults spent most of their time. I stayed in the pool with my two sons enjoying their fun and laughter. As usual, I had a lot on my mind. But being around them seemed to make everything in my world okay. It amazed me to see my daughter growing up. Now ten, she approached her mother's height and was no longer limited to swimming in the shallow end of the pool. With confidence, she ventured into the deep with no hesitation. After swimming, the kids enjoyed pizza and I had a chance to watch an NFL playoff game. Later that evening we all sang *Happy Birthday* to my daughter and enjoyed some cupcakes.

At night the girls went to their room and had a pillow fight. They stayed up laughing, watching television and two of them didn't fall asleep until six in the morning. My sons, their mother and I fell asleep way before them. After breakfast, the kids had a chance to swim for another hour before we checked out. In all, we had a good time and my daughter enjoyed her birthday. After dropping her classmate off at home, we all relaxed for a while at the main house not looking forward to work and school resuming the next day.

Later that week, I attended a work training seminar outside of the office. I received a phone call from my mortgage company and let it go to voicemail. I grew used to them calling me about the monthly payment being late, so I did not think anything of it. However, during my next break, for some reason I decided to call them back. My loan counselor answered with some disturbing news. She disclosed that, since last August, monthly payments on the mortgage had been 30 days late. She went on to state, if December's and January's payments were not made before the end of the month, that would make six consecutive months of payments being 30 days late and would put the loan into serious delinquency status. She urged me to make these two payments before the end of the month to avoid this from happening.

Upset about the news, I spoke to the mother of my children. She committed to making one payment before the end of January but not two. As frustrated as I felt about the situation, I saw no use bothering her anymore about it. With everything she was dealing with, the situation about the mortgage was not her biggest concern. I politely asked her to make the one payment she could. I knew January's payment would still be outstanding so I began filing her income taxes, hoping a tax refund would help cash flow issues.

I ran into yet another financial snag at the end of the month. I took my car in for a routine oil change and expected to spend no more than fifty dollars. During the inspection, the mechanic said I needed some additional work to be done. He recommended not putting it off, being the middle of winter. I grimaced at his recommendation but inquired about the cost. After checking my bank account, I authorized him to do the work having just enough to pay for everything.

I remember sitting in the waiting room as they worked on my car. My head began spinning thinking about all the upcoming bills, beginning next week with childcare and rent. I can't catch a break, I thought, considering how the unexpected auto repairs put me that much more in the hole financially. While there I text messaged my mother to see how she was doing. She responded, saying she and my father were both getting over colds. Besides that everything was okay. She inquired about me and I told her everything was fine and that I would call back the next day to check on them and further discuss a favor I needed.

The next afternoon I called my parents and it was a call I dreaded making. Even though they had helped me before, this time felt different. I was trying to do things on my own but still found myself needing help. My mother picked up the phone.

"Hello, Ma. How are you and Pop doing? Feeling better?" I asked.

"Son, we are okay just battling these colds. When you get older, it gets harder to shake them. That's why we hate getting sick," she replied. "So, what's up?"

"I hate to ask but I need another favor," I reluctantly said.

"Okay, give me one second and let me put your father on speaker phone so we can all discuss this," she replied.

"Yesterday, I took my car in for an oil change at Sears and ended up spending an additional three hundred dollars on a new tire rod, a wheel alignment and new wiper blades. Looking at what I have to pay in upcoming bills, I'm way short. I know I said I would try to handle things on my own financially, but I can't stay afloat. I always end up needing help. I feel like such a burden sometimes, I'm sorry," I sadly expressed.

My eyes watered. I felt so frustrated at my situation that I couldn't hold in my emotions any longer. I needed to cry and I did. A part of me was a little embarrassed but I was not trying to pretend for anyone, especially the two people who brought me into this world, loved and raised me.

After speaking with my parents they agreed to help me out. More importantly, they comforted me and told me everything would be alright. I needed their reassurance.

"Son, if you need anything we are always here," my father said.

Even as an adult, it felt wonderfully overwhelming to hear my parents say this. I was truly blessed to have them express this to me after all these years. They were my heroes and I knew GOD had sustained them for a reason. One of those being to comfort and support me at this crucial time in my life.

02.2017

month 12

With the help of my parents, I curbed a couple of financial jams. However, January's mortgage payment still hung over my head. I did not ask my parents for assistance in this matter, owning it as a dilemma the mother of my children and I had to work out. I just hoped the bank would not take action based on the payment still being delinquent.

Internally, I still fought the spiritual battle for control of my mind. Even though GOD was meeting my needs and I remained afloat, I could not mentally "let go" and believe that everything would work out. The basics of food, clothing, shelter, employment and transportation were continually provided. However, I found myself still perceiving the glass being half empty and not half full.

My mother happened to call the first weekend of the month to check on me. As we talked, she took control of the conversation and challenged me as a "so called" Christian and believer of the WORD OF GOD.

"Byron, you have been raised in church. You read and understand the Bible. You always seem to have good advice for others. Now, you need to follow you own advice and trust GOD. You know what HE has done in the lives of others and what HE has seen you through up until this point of your life," she said.

"You are right. I need to truly believe and follow my own advice," I replied.

"Now is the time for you to believe GOD fully. You need to embrace HIS WORD and stand on it. It's a new year and the season for doubt and unbelief has to end, if you are going to see GOD work in your life," she went on.

Her words connected with me as a fellow Christian and person in the faith, not as my mother. From that moment on, I told myself I would, "Let go and let GOD." The burdens I carried were too heavy for me. What I was in need of, I would depend on HIM to provide. Suddenly, my whole perspective began to change.

The Bible passages of *Matthew 11:28-30* and *Ephesians 2:8-9* renewed in my mind. I was mentally weary and needed rest. If it was by grace through faith that I received eternal salvation, not my own works or anything I could have done, then HIS grace was still sufficient to provide what I needed right now in this life, not my own works! I began to develop a different and better understanding of what it meant to "REST IN THE LORD."

I accepted things would change when GOD was ready and I had to wait on HIS TIMING. This was not easy to digest but I became convinced of this realization. If I needed a new job, I would wait on HIS direction and provision, even if that meant being still and not doing anything. I would no longer labor, looking and applying for jobs, when I did not know the next steps for my life. I had been doing this and it had not worked. There were thousands of jobs and hundreds of employers out there. How was I to know the right one for me? I didn't, so I needed to wait and trust HIS GUIDANCE and PROVISION. This belief released a huge burden off me.

Even though I had made up my mind to begin standing on HIS WORD, that did not mean things did not continue to come at me. That Monday, President's Day, was a routine morning. The weather was warm the night before and very pleasant for February. I woke up and made the kids breakfast and enjoyed a hot cup of coffee. With my children in the house, I went out to my car. Surprisingly, one of my back windows was busted out! Broken glass lay all over the back seat. It stunned me! In the past, I had dealt with break-ins. However, every time it happens you feel violated.

    I tried to calmly call the mother of my children and tell her what happened, that the kids and I would be delayed coming by the main house that day. I thought of the best way to clean up the glass and used a Kirby vacuum I had purchased the previous year. I told the kids to stay inside as I did not want them panicked by the broken glass. By the grace of GOD, the vacuum cleaned up everything and made the back seat safe for my sons.

    After cleaning up the car, I checked to see if anything was missing. Initially, I didn't think much was taken. I then walked around the backyard of the house and noticed a strange bicycle behind the garage. Turning back towards the house I also noticed that a couple of window screens had been cut. I decided to quickly get the kids dressed and out of the house. When my children approached the car, both of my sons noticed the broken window and asked what happened. My daughter then worriedly asked, "Have you seen my cell phone?" It was her first one, a white Samsung Galaxy S6 that she cherished.

    "No," I replied.

    "I left it in the car last night, on the front passenger seat," she said.

    I sadly explained that the phone must have been what the burglar saw and probably the main reason they broke into the car. She looked heartbroken and in disbelief about her stolen phone.

"How could someone just take my cell phone! Who gave them the right to do so!" she lamented.

On the way to the main house, I tried to console her and relay the message that life wasn't always right or fair. When we arrived I told the mother of my children about my daughter's phone. Of course, she was unhappy about the situation and called the cell phone company to see what insurances were on the plan and how much it would cost for a replacement. Since it was still early I began calling around to see who could fix my car window. I had the day off from work and didn't want to waste any time since the weather would be returning to normal, cold temperatures.

I spoke to a couple of window replacement companies and got some quotes on the repair. One of the companies gave me a return call after I had gotten off the phone with them. It was the company's manager and he explained that he could probably fix the window for a lot less than the initial quote just given. He politely asked what type of auto insurance I had and if it included comprehensive coverage. I gave him the information and he instructed me to go ahead and bring the car in. Before I got off the phone, I asked why he had been so polite.

"I've been in the auto glass repair business a long time and like to help people save money," he said. "If someone has insurance, why not help them use it."

I took it as a sign from GOD that HE remained right there with me in the midst of everything.

With my window fixed within a couple of hours, I returned home and called the police to file a report. An officer finally came after three hours and received a statement from me. He took the strange bike from behind the garage and went on his way in about ten minutes. It was a shame how nonchalant he was about the situation. However, burglaries happened all the time in the city. I re-secured all the windows of the house and slept that night on the couch in the family room by the side door, seemingly with one eye open. Before the kids were to spend the night at the house with me again, I needed to have some assurance the burglar would not return.

The next day things got more interesting. I received a notice from my mortgage lender in the mail. It said my loan was being recommended for foreclosure and I had ten days to reply with an acceptable payment plan or else they would begin the process. After informing the mother of my children about the notice and discussing the matter with her, I called my loan counselor and made a pitch to get the mortgage caught up by April.

She denied this request and told me, "The best I can do is give you until March to get the loan current." That meant a payment and a half would have to be made in February and March. These payments had to be mailed directly to her and received by the 28th of each month. I could no longer go to the local branch and make payments until the loan became current. She pleaded with me to honor the payment arrangement or there would be nothing else she could do.

Fortunately, the mother of my children's income tax refund was scheduled to arrive six days before the payment for February was due. Her ability to make the first payment required under the arrangement allowed us to dodge the first bullet. I told her to make sure she saved enough money to make the second payment due next month.

After dealing with these unexpected events much of my everyday life remained the same. I still received calls from debt collectors and formal notices in the mail. Some of my creditors began to offer me settlement options to deal with delinquent accounts. Another one of my delinquent accounts was sold to another lender. In knowing there was no way I could pay back the debt, my hope was to secure another job and then use my separation pay and money I could withdraw from a 403b retirement account to settle my debts for a portion of what I owed. I was not ready to file for bankruptcy yet as this would be my last resort. However, I did have apprehension that my creditors would soon begin to take legal action. The thought of this was frightening because I could not afford to be sued and have my wages garnished.

The month ended on an unsettling note for the mother of my children. Since January, she had been complaining about feeling lower abdominal pain that was intensifying. She went to see her doctor to find out that a problem, she hoped had been resolved last June in her surgical procedure, was re-occurring. She would need to have surgery again to deal with this issue. It seemed as if it wasn't one thing it was another but I had to learn to trust GOD through it all.

KEY VERSES

As it is written,

"Come unto me, all ye that labor and are heavy laden, and I will give you rest. Take my yoke upon you, and learn of me; for I am meek and lowly in heart: and ye shall find rest unto your souls. For my yoke is easy, and my burden is light."
Matthew 11:28-30

"For by grace are ye saved through faith; and that not of yourselves: it is the gift of God: Not of works, lest any man should boast."
Ephesians 2:8-9

03.2017

month 13

As a family we began to prepare for the mother of my children's surgery, scheduled for the last day of the month. The kids weren't thrilled that their mother needed another procedure. My daughter was especially frustrated about it. She did not like the fact her mother seemed ill all the time.

"Daddy, when is this going to stop? Is mommy ever going to get better?" she asked. She missed not being able to spend as much time with her mom. I tried to comfort and assure her that things would get better.

In the midst of everything going on, I began to notice and admire the resolve of my children and their mother. We all had been on a wild ride since last year. Despite the challenges, my children stayed upbeat and maintained their composure. They were doing well in school and did not complain as much as they could have. They rolled with the punches and I was proud of them. The same could be said for their mother. Her life both physically and mentally had been full of ups and downs the past year, but she kept hanging in there. We were learning to survive as a family.

During the month my oldest son attended another birthday party for one of his classmates at school. It seemed like every month someone invited him to a party. He was a very popular, likable young man. Luckily, his mother had purchased some inexpensive gifts from Target after the holidays that became very convenient for these parties. Along with the gift I would go to the dollar store and buy a greeting card, a small box of candy and a gift bag to put everything in. I would usually give him five dollars to put in the greeting card as well. I liked the kids to feel the touch of some money on their birthday.

My daughter began a new program called *Girls on the Run* at school. It was a ten week program designed to foster positive development while incorporating physical activity. My daughter met with her team twice a week after school. She truly needed this at the time. It allowed her to talk and discuss certain things that girls her age go through. The head coach of the team was a teacher at her school who had taught my oldest son in kindergarten. My daughter felt comfortable around her and developed some beneficial relationships with other girls on the team.

My daughter also received her new cell phone! Since our cell phone provider no longer carried the stolen phone, she received an upgrade. That made her joyful and I tried to use this circumstance as a teachable moment. I reminded her of how upset and down she got when first learning her old phone was stolen. However, after a little patience, she received a new, better phone. If she had not gone through the pain of losing the old phone, she would not have experienced the happiness and joy of receiving the new one. The scripture of *Romans 8:28* came to mind as I tried to remind myself that everything I was going through would work together for my good.

As the end of the month approached, the mother of my children paid the required mortgage payment due. With this now behind us, I was thankful and hoped to avoid this situation with the mortgage again. On the downside of things, my children weren't the only ones not thrilled about their mother being scheduled for another surgery. Her employer also was not happy. She had applied for FMLA leave earlier in the month but got denied. Since she had been out for a significant amount of time last year and had not worked enough hours since, she was not eligible.

Her employer did acknowledge her doctor's recommendation to have the procedure and granted her voluntary leave without pay. During her time off, she could not use any accrued vacation or sick time. For any time she missed, she would not get paid.

Initially, when hearing the response from her employer, the mother of my children considered not having the surgery. She was afraid to make the sacrifice financially and also feared losing her job.

"What if they try to fire me. I want to have the surgery but not lose my job," she expressed.

I reinforced the necessity of the procedure. She did not have a choice if the pain was to be treated. Others she relied on for advice told her the same thing. Her health and well-being was worth more than a paycheck. It would be tough, but we would have to make it work.

In foreseeing the mother of my children's financial situation getting tighter, I got anxious again and began to think about my employment situation. One night my fingers got itchy and I went onto the Indeed app on my phone. In the past, I would browse Indeed and LinkedIn when searching for job leads. I had gone five weeks without doing this and given my pursuit some rest. I saw a job with the Federal Reserve that looked really appealing and decided to apply.

With all that was going on, I still had some selfishness built up. The mother of my children was scheduled to have another surgery and here I was thinking about a job for myself. One that would benefit me financially, which in turn could benefit her. My thoughts seemed justified but they should have been in another place. I took for granted that everything would go fine with her procedure and life would go on normal from there.

As the surgery date approached I worked diligently to apply for the job with the Federal Reserve. To apply, I not only had to submit an online application with a resume and cover letter. I also had to submit a minimum five-page writing sample highlighting my credentials and qualifications. In putting together the writing sample, I did some research and pulled information from the Internet. Along with this, I had to word and sequence everything properly which took a lot of work. Nonetheless, I submitted the application.

The morning of the surgery I wasn't nervous. The mother of my children didn't appear overly anxious either. It was held in the same hospital with the same physician as the previous one. When we arrived at the hospital, she wanted to get prepped as soon as possible to get the procedure started and over with. Her parents were there and, as the surgery time approached, my anxiety heightened. Thoughts entered my mind. Had I taken this procedure for granted and what if something happens to her? There was no guarantee that everything would go well and I should have spent more time in prayer and given the situation the attention it deserved.

As I sat in the waiting room I tried to take my mind off things by doing some reading. This procedure ended up being shorter than the last one and, once again, my former mother-in-law and I had questions for the doctor when he came out. I tried harder to understand the pictures he brought out to show us regarding the surgery. Our main question was the elephant in the room.

"Would this surgery fix the problem or would it re-occur again?"

Of course, the doctor could not give us a full guarantee that the problem would not re-occur. He had done all he could and was satisfied where things stood. That was not the answer either of us wanted to hear, but we had to accept it as the best he could give at the time.

The mother of my children had made it through another surgery and I was hopeful this procedure would leave her better off than the previous one. I was also thankful for her doctor and his care and concern. The last couple of months had been really unpredictable but, as a family, we were surviving and embracing the possibility of change.

KEY VERSE

As it is written,

"And we know that all things work together for good to them that love God, to them who are the called according to his purpose."

Romans 8:28

04.2017

month 14

To begin the month the mother of my children spent two nights in the hospital before being released. She expressed her after surgery pain was intense but not as severe as the first time. She even developed an appetite soon after arriving home. Her first week home was quiet. She was able to rest and moved very well. However, she began to complain about some stomach pain.

We initially thought it was pain related to the surgery. She had been moving around and maybe had done too much, too early. We decided to take her to the emergency room at the hospital where the surgery was just performed. Unfortunately, after running some tests and monitoring her for two days, the doctors could not for sure tell what was wrong. They instructed her to follow up with one of the gastroenterologists at the hospital and her primary care physician. I felt uneasy about the situation and her father was also overly concerned, since she had just come home from the hospital a little over a week ago.

The Easter holiday followed. All five of us made the trip down to Kentucky to see my parents and, of course, the kids enjoyed being spoiled to the utmost. On Easter Sunday, all three of them participated in an egg hunt in my parents' backyard. The eggs were filled with one dollar bills and my oldest kids licked their chops in anticipation of an easy payday. I took advantage of their financial prosperity and made them pay for their own meals on the way home.

Financially, things were still tight. I still received calls from debt collectors but not as many as before. Since I decided to not answer or return any of their calls, they stopped harassing me as much. Even though I played possum on the phone, formal notices of delinquency still came via mail. I began to wonder why some of my creditors had not pursued further legal action yet. I figured GOD had to be on my side, somehow buying me time. Since I could not predict when my financial situation would turn around the idea of bankruptcy appealed more and more.

On some local highways and streets, I noticed bankruptcy representation advertisement for as low as six hundred dollars. That seemed very inexpensive to pay an attorney and many times you get what you pay for. I reached out to a family friend who worked in the legal field for some referrals. She sent me one referral of an attorney who she said was fair and reasonable. I decided to call the referral with nothing to lose. I called and scheduled an initial consultation for early next month. In between then I had to gather some financial information.

On a sad note, a member of the church I grew up in died. His funeral was April 22nd and despite being sluggish that Saturday morning, I attended out of respect for him and obeying a promise I made to my mother. He was a man, in his later years, who suffered from a chronic health condition. Regretfully, I had not seen him for a number of years. He was loved by a lot of people, especially the youth of our church. He served as the youth pastor and dedicated his life to pouring into young people.

His death served as another reminder of three things - life was short, time was passing by and I was getting older. Despite his death, I had joy in my heart knowing a triumphant afterlife awaited believers in JESUS

CHRIST called Heaven. A place where I could see him and others I loved and cherished once again - a place of happiness and not suffering. I thought about him, my grandparents and others being up there smiling and no longer concerned with the cares of this world. I looked forward to that glorious place one day!

KEY VERSE

As it is written,

"And God shall wipe away all tears from their eyes; and there shall be no more death, neither sorrow, nor crying, neither shall there be any more pain: for the former things are passed away."
Revelations 21:4

05.2017

month 15

May turned out to be a breakthrough month in a lot of ways! The weather warmed up and we began to score more victories. To begin, my youngest child began to use the bathroom on his own! What a huge triumph! Ever since he turned three his child care provider, his mother and I had been trying to get him to use the bathroom. However, he resisted and his mother and I grew concerned that he would not be ready to start preschool. Remaining calm, his child care provider assured us he would go when he was ready and we could not force it.

The interesting thing about this accomplishment was that my oldest son really got on me the previous month about it. One night, while trying to get my youngest one to sit on the potty and use the bathroom, he sat on it for ten minutes with no results. I tried to force the situation instead of letting it naturally happen.

"Nolan, why can't you go to the bathroom? What's wrong?" I asked in frustration.

After no luck that night, my oldest son taunted me saying my youngest was not listening and would never go to the bathroom on his own.

"Dad, you might as well give up. He is not listening to you. Ha Ha," he snickered jokingly.

At the time the situation with the potty did not look good. However, I trusted it would work out. When my oldest son surprisingly learned his younger brother had started using the bathroom, he innocently smirked at me with nothing to say. His younger brother's actions had shut him up. I reminded him of what he had previously said about the situation and how he was mistaken. At the time of his initial comment, he appeared to be right. But, over time, he became wrong. Not only was his younger brother urinating in the toilet, he also began pooping in it later in the month. Diapers became a thing of the past and gladly no longer an expense our family had to worry about.

In addition, I had my initial consultation with the bankruptcy attorney. A short lady with a lot of energy, you could tell she had a lot of enthusiasm for her job. I liked seeing that in someone who could potentially be representing me. After reviewing the financial information I provided her, she said I qualified for bankruptcy. She explained the different bankruptcy options available and the timetable for filing. I inquired about what would happen to the house I still owned and had a mortgage, where my children and their mother resided. I did not want them displaced. She explained what would happen to the house and told me to think things over. She informed me that she would be out of the country the following week and would not be back until the end of the month. Upon her return, if I wanted to file, I should contact her.

Also, the mother of my children had her initial consultation with a different gastroenterologist to get a second opinion on the stomach pain she was experiencing. The new doctor, a female, was more caring about understanding her condition and discussing the best way to treat it.

"She seems to really care about me as a person and not just a patient," the mother of my children happily expressed.

Up until that point, she had a male, foreign doctor. At times, she struggled to understand his speech, which made communicating with him difficult. In addition, his appointment times always ran late. When she would finally get in to see him, she felt rushed. As a result, she was really uncomfortable about eating anything and really did not want to talk much about the situation. The new doctor gave her hope that she could find results to treat her condition properly.

The following day, my daughter had her spring 5k marathon with her *Girls on the Run* team. The race was held at a destination about an hour away, so we had to be up and out early. Her aunt and I raced with her to provide moral support and make sure she finished. It was my first 5k and I wanted to prove to myself that I could finish that long of a distance. That morning temperatures were in the high 50s which made great weather for running. All three of us finished and I was most proud of my daughter for sticking it out. She had fulfilled her commitment for the program and conquered the marathon.

While all these great things occurred, I still had one main issue hanging over my head. The issue of mortgage payments on the main house had arose again, being a problem we could not get under control. Due to the recent surgery in March, the mother of my children had missed work and her income declined. The mortgage payment for April was past due and May's payment was also owed. We had just climbed out of a deep rut to get the loan current through March and now faced another one.

I tried not to think about it too much. However, I did not know how the issue would get resolved this time. I feared the bank would prepare to foreclose on the house without giving us an opportunity to bring the loan current as before. The mother of my children was aware of the issue and I left it with her. I was due to receive an extra paycheck from work at the end of May that could possibly pay one month. However, I decided not to do this. I had to let the situation play out without my interference and let the mother of my children find a way to resolve it.

She lived in the house so the mortgage was hers to pay, a responsibility she had struggled with ever since taking it on. If she could not afford to pay, maybe it was best to let the house go and try to sell it. I wondered how my oldest two kids could potentially be affected since they loved the school they attended. However, I stuck to my guns and stayed out of the situation.

All my worrying was to no avail! Somehow, the mother of my children came up with the money to pay both months. I did not try to figure out how she came up with the money or who helped her. I did not need to know how she accomplished this miraculous feat. All I knew was the situation worked out without me being involved. Consequently, on the last day of the month, I received an unexpected two-day shut off notice for a delinquent water bill at the rental house. Since I did not get involved in the situation with the mortgage, I was financially able to resolve the entire balance of this bill and keep my services on. GOD once again provided, this time in both our situations!

The month closed on a high note. With the second major hurdle concerning the mortgage cleared, going forward, I told myself I would no longer worry about the mortgage payment on the main house. GOD would somehow provide! HE once again proved that HE was with me and my family in the midst of everything that we were facing. We were surviving and had scored some victories with the expectation more were forthcoming.

06.2017

month 16

The month of June started off great! Summer was in full bloom and my parents surprisingly came into town. The first Friday of the month I talked with them about and the idea of filing for bankruptcy. After fielding their questions, they agreed to give me the money needed to hire the attorney. I then took my father out to eat some chicken wings. He loved eating them as we enjoyed the time drinking beer and catching up on the restaurant's patio.

Also, the mother of my children paid the mortgage payment owed for June on time. This was the first month she had been able to do this. I felt relieved this task was already taken care of, which helped the month flow a lot easier. For the first time since last July, I did not have to worry about when the mortgage would be paid.

On Sunday morning, my parents were scheduled to leave and they wanted to see the grandchildren. The children were with their mother and the four of them had gone out for breakfast. There was some confusion about what time they would return and also what time my parents wanted to come by the main house and see them. When noon came around my parents were ready to leave but I asked them to wait and meet up with everyone at the main house.

When I arrived, my parents were already inside talking to the kids and their mother. I politely asked the children to go upstairs, as the four adults needed to talk. I started the conversation by thanking everyone for their role over the past year. I acknowledged that many changes had occurred and, without the support of everyone involved, my family would not have been able to sustain. However, I had to address the tension between my parents and the mother of my children.

This tension existed even while we were married. I knew my parents believed our marriage was not the best decision. They weren't surprised it struggled and did not survive. At times, during our marriage, I felt my parents were judgmental towards my then wife and accepted her only because of me and the children. However, I believed they were not always fond of her partly because of the way she treated me.

The mother of my children had made some mistakes. However, I had made some too. One of mine being not supporting her enough by standing up to my parents on her behalf. As her then husband I was supposed to protect her, even from family members of mine who may have felt indifferent towards her and our relationship. With all the tension built up over the years and with everything my family had gone through the past year, I could not sit back and hold my tongue any longer.

I expressed to my parents that the mother of my children would always be that, their mother. Even though we were no longer married, she was still a part of this family and I wanted them to continue regarding her in that way. I wanted the lines of communication to remain open between them and her and for there to be no confusion about how I felt about this issue. The mother of my children chimed in.

"I would never try to keep your parents from seeing their grandchildren," she said.

"We appreciate that," my mother replied. "Please remember we have been there for you two and these children from the beginning. We love and want the best for all five of you."

Thankfully, the conversation ended gracefully and everyone agreed to do better going forward. My parents stayed for a while longer and said goodbye to the kids before departing. I gave both of them huge hugs as they left and told them I loved them. They returned the same greeting and pulled out of the driveway.

"Thank you for standing up for me," the mother of my children said.

"No problem," I replied, knowing I did the right thing.

Despite our marital status she remained my children's mother and I loved and supported her. I needed for my parents and her to know that.

The following Thursday proved to be another uplifting day for my family. Both of my oldest children had softball games and came home with victories and smiles. My son was accompanied to the game by his mother, who was quick to tell me he hit a grand slam home run! He also received his softball pants and cleats earlier that day, so he felt like a real player with the success he had enjoyed on the field. I accompanied my daughter to her game and her team also won with the final score being 7 to 6. She scored the winning run by taking a walk to get on base.

After the game the coaches huddled with the team and surprisingly awarded her the game ball! My daughter's look was priceless and she felt so accomplished, even though she was one of the more average players on the team. Her coaches congratulated the girls on their victory and announced practice for that coming Saturday.

Saturday morning came and my daughter wasn't in the mood to go practice. I shared her sentiment in having to take her. When we arrived at the field the coaches weren't there and some of the girls were still trickling in. Fifteen minutes passed and still no sign of the coaches. The girls had begun playing catch but, due to having limited equipment, they could only do some catching and throwing drills. Practice was led by one of the parents and lasted for an hour. My daughter was upset that her coaches did not show. She complained about them the whole ride home and I felt her frustration.

"How could they call a practice and not show?" she asked. "They wasted everyone's time and if we don't practice, we won't get better," she said. After their win earlier in the week, this practice could have really helped the team gain some momentum.

When the mother of my children heard about the no show of the coaches she called the Board President of the softball league. The Board President was surprised to hear about the no show and stated that was not behavior he expected from league coaches. He assured the mother of my children that he would look into the situation. On Monday, we received some shocking news. The three coaches of my daughter's softball team were murdered! All the families of the team were in shock!

I just saw these three ladies, four short days ago, and could not believe this had happened. All I could remember was the smile of one of the coaches, as she presented my daughter with the game ball. That smile was the last memory I had of her for the short time we knew each other. It was a pleasant memory and I was once again reminded of how short life was. You could be living one day and dead the next.

The girls had a game scheduled the next day and, of course, no one felt like playing. The league cancelled the game and the neighborhood Councilman, the Board President and two grievance counselors showed up at the field for anyone who needed to talk. The reaction reminded me of the reason why my kids no longer enjoyed listening to the radio in the morning. It seemed daily someone was reported being killed and they were tired of hearing about death on the news. It was eye opening that my three young children, especially the oldest two, began to view death as a common thing. Something that just happened randomly to people, sometimes without any real rhyme or reason. I too began to view death differently.

After that Tuesday, the girls looked defeated. However, it didn't take long for some angels to come to their rescue. By the weekend new coaches were found and a dynamic new player as well! Believe it or not, the girls had a good practice that Saturday and their attitude brightened. They had a game scheduled the following Monday, but the weather prevailed and it got rained out.

That evening I left early from the main house and the kids spent the night with their mother. Since I had some spare time I stopped inside a grocery store. I then darted in and out of a Dollar Tree and headed up the street on my way home. While at a stop light, I heard another car beeping across from me.

Behind the wheel sat someone I had not seen in a while, an old friend who worked in the human resources field. She looked happy and smiled the whole time we talked at the light. I asked if she had the same phone number and she replied "yes." I spoke with her the next evening and learned why she was so happy. Of course, it wasn't just because she saw me.

She had landed a new job as Director of Human Resources for a local agency. It was the dream position for her made possible from an old contact she knew. She recounted how she was not even aware the position was available until her old contact reached out. The contact was about to retire but informed her about the position before doing so.

She told me she wasn't really looking for a job at the time. She had two kids in college and was content sticking it out at her then present job for needed financial stability. She told herself that she would be open to change if the right opportunity came along, even if it meant changing retirement systems. However, she was not looking for a new job at the time.

Her talking to me that night was really encouraging. I could not help but to think of my own employment situation and how I had been waiting for change. I was not selected for an interview for the last position I applied for in March, but listening to her and her testimony let me know GOD was still with me in my situation. Even though I had not received any results, HE was still able to turn things around.

Not only had my friend obtained the top working title in her field, she obtained the position at an agency that carried the same retirement plan! She could retire in less than ten years making a higher salary and working less hard at this new position than some of her previous ones. I was happy for her and it confirmed for me the true goodness of GOD!

GOD had to be blowing in my direction because the next day at work I received an email from an unexpected source about a job opportunity! The source was a lady who I had come to know and appreciate. A couple years ago, she wrote a letter of recommendation on my behalf for another position. Even though I did not get the job, I thanked her and asked that she keep me in mind for other positions.

The last time I spoke to her about keeping an eye open for me was last December. For her to remember after six months had to be GOD'S doing! I promptly opened her email and reviewed the available position at hand. It was with a community bank that I had never heard of. The bank was hiring for a Community Development Relationship Manager position in the Cleveland, Ohio area.

The bank had been hiring for this position all across their national service area and the Cleveland position was the only one left unfilled.

"This has to be the position I have been waiting for!" I thought to myself. The position offered the potential for a sizable increase in pay and in addition would allow me to spend more time out of the office interacting with community stakeholders and businesses. I could not believe my prayers were finally being answered! I thankfully replied and informed her that I would be applying for the position and would keep her abreast on what happened.

My outlook got even better the next day. I submitted everything necessary for my attorney to file the bankruptcy petition. To say that I was on cloud nine would be an understatement! I shifted from being "the hunted" to "the hunter." Once my creditors received notice of the filed petition, I knew they could no longer contact me about my outstanding debts. If they did, I could redirect them to my attorney for any questions. The most they could do was attend the meeting of creditors and object to the discharge. With the bankruptcy filing, I could now see my way out of the deep hole I had dug for myself with personal debt.

The month concluded with me formally submitting my resume and applying for the position with the community bank. Upon submission, the recruiter scheduled a time for us to talk briefly over the phone. The phone conversation went well and from there a Skype interview was scheduled, which also went favorably. After the interview, I was told to wait a couple weeks to hear back concerning next steps.

The month of June was another wild ride! There were some very unexpected tragedies and also some unexpected victories. I finally seemed to receive personal breakthroughs and felt answers to my uncertainties had surfaced. I felt my plane starting to get some lift as I could see myself coming out of my wilderness experience and making it to the other side.

07.2017

month 17

July began with the national Independence Day holiday. But first, my daughter had a double header of softball games to play the first Sunday of the month. A lot of the parents weren't thrilled about two games being scheduled on the same day during the holiday weekend. I shared their sentiment but, due to the weather, previous scheduled games were cancelled. The team needed to make these games up with the playoffs starting in less than two weeks.

That afternoon was hot and humid. Both games were against a team that had whooped the girls pretty bad earlier in the season. Their opponent was the best in their division and the girls knew it. However, since the new coaches came on board, the level of expectancy had risen. The new coaches lived and breathed youth athletics and they weren't going to accept any kind of effort from the team. They expected the girls to compete and win.

In the first game, the girls did compete but came up short just one run. During the break between games, even though they had lost, you could tell the girls were filled with confidence heading into game two. They were determined to take the second game and believed they had earned the respect of their opponent. The parents and coaches were also confident of a victory in game two.

However, as the second game progressed, the girls seemed to lose their competitive edge. Maybe the humid weather played a part. They were down five runs with only two innings left. In the dugout they appeared unfocused, lacking the desire to give the extra effort to turn things around. Despite how the second game progressed my daughter never lost her drive. The coaches and I both noticed how she continued to hustle, jogging swiftly out to the outfield and into the dugout in between innings.

The captain of my daughter's team ended up getting a big hit that sparked a huge bottom next inning for the team! This was very encouraging since, earlier in the game, she had a verbal quarrel with her mother, who was one of the coaches. That hit and momentum carried over to the last inning of the game where the girls came back and won 14 to 12! It was a team effort led by its leading players on a hot, humid day to get the victory. The girls gained confidence and beat a team they once feared. Going into the playoffs, they now knew they could compete and possibly beat this opponent again.

In this huge win surprisingly the game ball was once again awarded to my daughter! I was surprised as much as anyone of her selection. However, the coaches acknowledged her consistent hustle throughout the game - even when the team was losing was important to their victory. The coaches went on to reinforce that this type of consistency, in practices and in games, would lead to more victories. As the team and parents celebrated, the coaches' message regarding consistency stuck in my mind.

It reminded me of how far I had come over the past seventeen months. How a lot of that time I was down and felt like giving up. However, I had to continue to consistently pray and feed my faith nourishment and not doubt. My nourishment continually was the WORD OF GOD, the channels of Christian radio and television and everyday life experiences such as the second game on Sunday, July 2nd. In all that I observed and heard, I could sense the presence of GOD.

On the Fourth of July, my son was involved in a morning parade with the local Boy Scout troop. We were all up early to get good seats and witness the parade. The streets were filled with people from all walks of life: children, seniors, churches, veterans, politicians, businesses and marching bands. There were plenty of smiles to commemorate the holiday. That night we watched some fireworks and were mindful of the time because the mother of my children was scheduled to return to work the next day from her medical leave. She dreaded returning but, out of necessity, didn't have an choice.

I tried to encourage her in knowing she had enjoyed the time off so much. She got a chance to spend more time with the kids, which in turn gave me more of a break. Her returning to work would mean the kids would resume spending most of the nights with me again. I wasn't upset only thankful for the break I had received.

Later in the month I learned the recruiter was submitting me for consideration for the job! I felt exceptionally zealous for this opportunity and took the news, with expectation, that things were continuing to progress and that my long awaited change was inevitable. It seemed all signs were pointing in that direction as well. At work, I saw a fellow colleague of mine coming down the steps on the way to a meeting.

"When's your last day?" he coincidently asked.

I gave a real casual response in not having any news to announce yet. However, I kept a mental note of his foresight into my certain change.

The month concluded with the meeting of creditors for my bankruptcy petition. When my attorney and I arrived at the courthouse and got off the elevator, we walked into a crowded lobby area. It was surprising to see how many people were seeking the same type of financial relief. The meeting was scheduled for 10:30 a.m. but we didn't make it in to see the bankruptcy trustee until 11:00 a.m.

None of my creditors showed for the meeting. The trustee asked some general questions concerning my employment, my house and the filing of the previous year's income taxes. Under oath, I answered when needed and the hearing ended in approximately twenty minutes. The trustee granted my bankruptcy petition! I walked out of the courthouse excited but still inquired with my attorney about anything else that needed to be done.

"Within eight weeks you should receive a notice of final discharge from the court. However, up until that time, your creditors have a chance to challenge the discharge, but I don't see the likeliness of that happening," she said.

As I walked back to my car, I thought about how blessed I truly was! Leading up to the bankruptcy filing, for months, I pondered how I would resolve all the personal debt that was weighing me down. The amount of debt I owed was in the thousands! For me to be able to walk away and not owe these obligations anymore was mind blowing.

Yes, my credit history would be stained. However, a huge burden had been lifted. I would have never imagined seventeen months ago that I would take the route of bankruptcy. However, the opportunity it offered me to start fresh was an invaluable one. As July ended, I continued down the road of faith amassing blessings along the way!

08.2017

month 18

August kicked off with a seventh birthday party for my oldest son. Excitement filled the air as it was an occasion he'd been looking forward to for at least six months. We held the party at a laser tag arena full of fun and games. My son got a chance to catch up with a lot of his school friends whom he missed over the summer. I played a couple of laser tag games myself. Running through the dark, lit maze brought back fond memories. The enjoyment was twice as nice in spending time with my children and their friends. I was once again reminded of how blessed my life truly was. I didn't have money but love was near.

Later in the month my daughter had her own sense of enjoyment by going out of town with her aunt and cousin. They traveled to North Carolina for an enjoyable getaway. My daughter got a chance to see family, eat at various restaurants and go swimming. The trip was all smiles. I thanked her aunt for furnishing my daughter's mini vacation. She was also polite enough to take my two oldest children out of town earlier in the summer. With money being so tight, the mother of my children and I were not able to afford a family vacation. Their aunt stood in the gap and supplied some much needed summer enjoyment for my kids.

With a new school year on the horizon the end of summer rapidly approached. The change of seasons was coming and I began to think of the anticipated changes forthcoming in my life. I tried not to be too anxious about the job. I had not heard anything further from the recruiter. Only that I was still in consideration for the position and updates regarding next steps in the hiring process were taking longer than expected. I tried to remind myself that patience was the key and, if meant to be, it would happen. In the midst of delays, I remained convinced the job was mine – no ifs, ands or buts about it.

However, it was difficult for me not to think about the timing of being hired and the potential pay increase the new position could bring. Even with the granted bankruptcy, I still had a main financial issue that needed to be addressed. The rear roof at the main house needed to be replaced. When purchasing the house seven years ago, the inspection noted that the whole roof was approaching the end of its usable life. I managed to get the front side of the roof replaced two years into buying the house.

However, the rear was on its last legs. I was fortunate enough to get through the snow and ice of the past winter without having any major problems. However, during the rainy seasons of spring and summer, water started to seep through rotted wood and deteriorated shingles into the main bedroom upstairs, as water spots surfaced on the ceiling. I knew the roof would not survive another winter and I did not have the estimated $3,200 needed to have it replaced.

Just like everything else, I had to try and remain calm and trust it would work out. In the meantime, I had to enjoy everyday life and the joys and experiences that came with it. Another one of those joys included the end of season party for my daughter's softball team. The event took place at a local park on a sunny, but not overwhelmingly hot day. It was a fun time between families with a common bond. There was a host of food, beverages and the girls also received trophies. The highlight of the party was the kids versus parents softball game! Of course us over the hill parents won and the girls claimed we cheated. Talks of a rematch were hatched and it was a fun and great way to celebrate their season.

Their season ended on a bittersweet note. Excitedly, the girls made it to the championship game in the playoffs! Unfortunately, they lost by one run to the opponent they split the double header with in July. The loss really left a bad taste in their mouths being so close.

However, no one could deny the season they had and how they persevered through all the ups and downs. Watching them recover like they did to go on and make the playoffs, then advance to almost winning the championship was just another sign of how mystifying life could be. Their softball season was a testimony that GOD could take an adverse, rock bottom situation and turn it around for good.

Another joy came at the end of the month as my two oldest children started a new school year. Their mother and I both went into work late that day and treated the kids to a sit down breakfast. As a tradition, we always liked to spend this time with them on the first day. We also accompanied them to school and met their teachers. As parents we wanted them and their teachers to know we took their education seriously.

As the month came to a close, I had learned to enjoy everyday life again and the morsels of happiness and fulfillment it offered. I had come to accept that my long awaited change would come at the proper time. Until then I had an obligation to continue to take care of myself and others GOD had bestowed in my care.

09.2017

month 19

September was another chance to really enjoy friends and family. Within the month I took two trips which were both overdue. The first was a voyage traveling to Virginia to see my brother and his family. It was Labor Day weekend and I took all three kids with me. My daughter was most pleased since she had been pleading with me to go see her uncle. It worked out that my brother was available that weekend and my parents graciously gave me some money to help with traveling expenses.

As I filled up the gas tank that Saturday morning, my mind began to think about how long it had been since I spent a weekend at my brother's house. When he first relocated to Virginia my daughter was very young and he was not married with a family. I used to make it down to see him at least twice a year. Over time, as he got married and our families expanded, it was harder for us to get together. I was happy to be making the familiar drive to Virginia again.

The weekend was very relaxing and my kids enjoyed the different landscape Virginia had to offer. The various housing and retail developments had a different feel than back home. My daughter made me vow to bring them back more often.

"Daddy, I want to come here for Labor Day every year. That will be the holiday we spend with Uncle Norm and his family," she said.

"If possible, I will. I promise."

Upon returning home, my mind began to shift to Viva Las Vegas! I had not been there since March of last year. This time I was going with some friends to celebrate one of their birthdays. This trip had been discussed a year in advance and I promised then I would go. At the time I thought my financial situation would for sure be better. However, when the travel arrangements were made, I could not afford my plane ticket. In bailing me out, my friend's wife willingly paid for my ticket showing me their true friendship.

The trip to Vegas would allow me to get some much needed rest and relaxation. As much as I loved my kids, a whole five days without them sounded unthinkable! Before leaving for the trip I had to pay a moving violation ticket for speeding and not wearing my seat belt. The fine was in excess of two hundred dollars which put a big dent in my spending money for Vegas. It was my first ticket in over three years and I wasn't happy about it! I had strategically maneuvered how I would pay my bills just to have enough money available for the trip. Regardless of this disappointing setback, I remained determined to have a great time.

At work, the week I was scheduled to leave for Vegas, my immediate supervisor called me into his office. He spoke to me about a new initiative the organization would be launching and the role my department would play in it. The department would be assigned new duties and this would result in more work for our section and me. Due to this additional responsibility, he instructed me to formally submit a letter requesting an increase in pay.

Initially, I had mixed feelings about submitting the request. Yes, this would represent a financial increase and I should have felt fortunate, especially the way I had struggled financially. However, because I felt I had been underpaid for some time and that a raise was long overdue, I was not as enthused as I should have been. Plus, the job I was still in consideration for remained in the forefront of my mind.

"What was the point of submitting for a pay increase if I would be leaving the organization soon anyways?" I said to myself.

However, in obedience to my supervisor, I put in the request for an increase with nothing to lose. I submitted a formal letter to my immediate supervisor and the Director of my department. In the letter, I described how I had been in my current position for six years and still was underpaid in comparison to my predecessor. That despite receiving quality performance reviews and being told informally from office colleagues that my work was superior, I still had not been increased to the same salary. I had only received standard cost of living increases when they were offered by the organization.

I went on to state that other department managers had received pay increases and that another employee in the department was promoted to management with increased pay with less than two years of work history with the organization. I concluded the letter respectfully with the requested amount of salary increase. After writing the letter, my mind angrily reflected on how I had been underappreciated by my current employer.

Despite the way I felt, I was proud of and respected myself for maintaining a sound, consistent level of morale. The Bible passage of *Ephesians 6:5-8* came to mind as I had truly served my department. When the time came for me to leave, my supervisor could not be upset. I had served from the heart despite not always receiving the support from him I should have through the years. I was ready to depart but remained committed to continue doing my job as accustomed until that time came. I wanted to sprint through the finish line not just cross it.

Later that week the flight to Las Vegas was early in the morning and scheduled to take approximately four and a half hours. It ended up being one of the smoothest flights I ever boarded. Upon takeoff, the plane maintained altitude and floated turbulence free. I fell asleep a couple of times and was not awakened by any shaking or awkward movements. We arrived earlier than anticipated and the trip was off to a great start!

For five days we laughed, talked and enjoyed each other's company. We did some exploring and toured parts of Las Vegas that were new to me. This was only my third trip to Vegas. The first two were shorter and, by the time I got comfortable, it was time to leave. This time it felt like I was there long enough to do everything I could afford. I felt blessed to have been able to make the trip. While there I did not think about normal life back home. My mind left any unresolved issues on hold until I returned.

As the trip wound down I promised myself that if I ever returned to Vegas, I would stay long enough to make it worthwhile like this experience. I enjoyed myself and had a chance to meet some interesting people. Most importantly, my friend had a likewise experience and really enjoyed his birthday.

Within a week of returning home I received exciting news. The recruiter contacted me and stated that next steps were in play as the community bank was finally ready to begin the interviewing process! This was really encouraging considering, while away, my immediate supervisor and Director had a conversation about the formal letter I submitted. The discussion centered on how much of an increase I should receive. I was upset and felt any meeting about my request should have included me in it. I would have preferred the opportunity to speak for myself. The fact that they had a meeting while I was gone did not sit well with me.

As a result of the meeting, I was told an increase would be included for me in the preliminary budget for next year. However, the increase would not happen until the budget passed next year and the appropriate paperwork was finalized. Thus, my increase was conditional on certain things happening, certain things I did not know for sure would happen. With that being said, I locked in an interview time during the second week of October. My confidence that change was near increasingly grew.

KEY VERSE

As it is written,

"Servants, be obedient to them that are your masters according to the flesh, with fear and trembling, in singleness of your heart, as unto Christ; Not with eyeservice, as menpleasers; but as the servants of Christ, doing the will of God from the heart; With good will doing service, as to the Lord, and not to men: Knowing that whatsoever good thing any man doeth, the same shall he receive of the Lord, whether he be bond or free."
Ephesians 6: 5-8

10.2017

month 20

As the month started, I only thought about the upcoming job interview. The date was set for the 10th at 10 a.m., to be held at a local hotel near the airport. The week before the interview I received more wonderful and relieving news. The notice of final discharge for my bankruptcy arrived in the mail and I could finally put those debts and the financial heartache they caused totally behind me! I solemnly swore to myself that I would never entrap myself in debt like that again.

Leading up to the interview I tried not to be too nervous. I remained confident that the job was mine and maintained this calm approach as the day drew near. I did ask the recruiter for any advice he could lend. He told me to be myself and to display enthusiasm and confidence. With that being said, I felt very assured the morning of the interview. I put on one of my newer dress shirt and tie combinations with a conventional blue blazer and headed out the door. The mother of my children kindly sent me a text message wishing me good luck. Her support meant a lot and I welcomed and appreciated it. Upon arriving at the location, I parked my car and prayed before entering the hotel.

The interviewers were running behind so I had ten minutes or so to unwind. Once they arrived, another five minutes was needed for them to get settled. They finally called me in and the dialogue began. I entered a conference room with a brown wooden table and sat at the head with one interviewer on both sides of me.

Both were men who had been with the hiring agency for over ten years. They talked about the positive culture of the organization and I learned that the wife of one of the interviewers worked for the organization as well. I spoke about my work experience as they wanted to know my approach to the area of community development. I also explained what drew me to pursue this opportunity with the organization and how I found out about the job opening.

As the interview unfolded it felt more like an easy-going conversation. A whole hour passed and it seemed like we could have talked for another. As the interview concluded, I asked about next steps and the timetable for hiring. They informed me that another round of interviews would be held and, if selected, some travel may be required. I politely thanked them for their time and wished them safe travels on their departure the next day. As I walked back to my car, I knew that I had left a good impression. I was confident that I would be selected to advance to the next interview round.

My excitement from the interview carried over into the weekend. Late Sunday afternoon, I drove to the main house to pick up the kids and see if their mother needed any assistance. Upon my arrival, she welcomed me inside and led me upstairs. To my pleasant surprise, when we reached the doorway to my daughter's room I stood there in true amazement. The room had been totally transformed, cleaned and organized! The mother of my children had managed to conquer the insurmountable task of cleaning my daughter's bedroom.

In awe, I asked "What made you clean the room?"

"I got tired of seeing it the way it was," she said. "Every time I pass by Olivia's room it looks awful. I got tired of asking her to clean it, so I decided to do it myself."

Her response was truly gratifying. Despite her constant battle with being physically tired, she mustered up enough energy and concern to address this issue. This was a huge task and victory that I could not have been more proud and appreciative of! I firmly instructed my daughter to not let her room get like that again as she now had an example of how to properly clean it. Later that night, I was still in amazement of what the mother of my children had accomplished.

Then the month grew exceedingly above and beyond what I could ask or think! When I got off of work on the 17th, I headed over to the main house as usual. When I arrived the mother of my children told me to go to the next street over and speak to a roofing contractor, who was currently installing a new roof on someone's house. I did not know why she told me to do this, but I listened and went over to the next street as instructed. I talked with one of the workers and received the owner's business card.

A couple mornings later I spoke with the owner and discussed his price and availability to replace the rear roof. He stated the job could be completed in one day and that he was available over the weekend. The price would be $3,600 which seemed very reasonable due to the fact another contractor quoted the same job, only $400 less, five years ago. I told him I would get back with him shortly and then text messaged the mother of my children asking if she had the money for the job.

"No," she replied. I then asked her to call me, which she did.

"Hello, thanks for calling so quickly. Be honest, can you afford to pay for the roof to get fixed?" I asked.

"I wasn't being dishonest," she replied. "I can afford to pay $2,000 once the job is completed and the additional $1,600 two weeks from then. Please call the owner back and see if he is willing to accept these payment terms," she said.

I called the owner back and he accepted our terms! He came by that evening and we formalized everything with an executed work proposal. By the 22nd, his company tore off the old rear roof and replaced it! I did not see this coming at all. It, once again, proved that GOD WAS IN THE MIDST OF OUR SITUATION!

To receive this awesome victory the only work I did was inquire about the roof work being done. Within my initial inquiry, the work was completed in only five days! GOD had provided through the mother of my children to have this burden lifted from me. It was so unexpected because she also had been struggling financially. I did not have to come up with any extra money as this major expense was now resolved.

As this triumphant month ended, I received word from the recruiter that I would in fact be moving to the next interview round! This round would serve as the final interview. After it concluded, a hiring decision would be made. Excited to hear the news, I just knew the position was mine! I had made it this far and was convinced there was no room for rejection.

11.2017

month 21

When November began I was eagerly waiting to hear back from the recruiter on a date for the final interview. Things began to speed up mentally for me as I realized this could be it! I was finally nearing the end of my journey to new, more promising employment. However, the excitement actually began on the first evening of the month as parent teacher conferences were held at my oldest children's school. GOD once again reminded me to stay in the moment and enjoy everyday life!

My daughter received great compliments from both her teachers on her work ethic, behavior and leadership qualities. The same day of the conference my oldest son received a "meets expectation" grade on his third module math test. He could not wait to show me his test as he sported a big grin when I walked through the door.

"Dad, I have a surprise to show you, look, look, look!" he excitedly said.

I was happy and pleased as we had worked tirelessly leading up to the test to make sure he had a sound understanding of everything. The much improved grade was extremely encouraging because he really struggled on the first two module tests. Later that evening, his teacher said she could tell he worked hard preparing for the test. As we walked down the hallway exiting the school, we ran into the school principal. I asked her how both of my kids were doing and she calmly replied, "No worries."

I walked out of the school a very proud father. I knew my daughter's improvement from last school year to this one was in part a testament of how hard I stressed the importance of listening in class and completing her homework. Reflecting back, I remember many nights that I would stay up with her working on homework. We would try to figure things out together and I stressed the importance of asking her teachers questions while in class. That discipline was starting to bear fruit and let me know my efforts with my children were being rewarded. Above anything else I envisioned for myself to achieve, being a good father was something I wanted to continue to be committed too.

The following week, I heard from the recruiter and he inquired about doing the interview in Philadelphia, PA on Tuesday the 21st at 3 p.m. Initially, I was not happy to have to travel such a long distance. This would all have to take place during the week of Thanksgiving and the price of airfare would be at a premium. Plus, I had planned on leaving the following day Wednesday headed to Kentucky for the holiday.

However, the recruiter told me the interview had to take place in Philadelphia. There were no other options. He also told me my travel expenses would be fully reimbursed, so I accepted. Without delay, I was able to borrow the money and reserve the air travel with the intention of arriving in Philadelphia and flying home the same day.

The next day started out business as usual and I was relieved to have the flight arrangements for the interview secured. I suddenly received a phone call from the mother of my children while a work. Due to budget constraints, she was being laid off from her employer! She was surprised and upset while crying on the telephone.

"It hurts! How could they treat me like this after ten years?" she cried.

I tried to calm her down and offer some encouragement and reassurance that everything would be okay. She listened to me for a couple of minutes before ending the call. She then emailed me the formal notice confirming her lay off, which went into effect that day. The rest of her last day was spent gathering up personal belongings and loading them into her car.

As I began to reflect on what just happened, I realized it was a true blessing in disguise. The mother of my children would be better off not working there any longer. She not only disliked going to work but was also unhappy with the overall direction of the organization. Under new leadership, the organization had changed and was causing her more anxiety and stress. Many days she would grudgingly go to work and the tension from her job contributed to her lack of sleep at night. She would wake up tired and miserable and have to do it all over again.

Due to the toll of her job, we had discussed her walking away from it and figuring out something else financially. She said that she would seriously consider doing so sometime early next year. However, I knew the mother of my children. She would not have willingly walked away. Her fear of being without money would have kept her stuck there, even if she needed to leave. Now, there was no decision to ponder. GOD made the decision for her and closed the door.

In making that decision, GOD also provided provision. She would still be paid for the rest of the month and afterwards be eligible for unemployment compensation. Her income would be affected but it was worth the trade of being able to let that stressful situation go. She would be able to get more rest, spend more time with the children and in turn lighten my burden. I was relieved and once again I knew GOD remained in the midst of our situation!

As the date of the job interview approached, the recruiter reached out to see if I had taken care of my flight arrangements. I confirmed with him and surprisingly he reached out to me again on the 17th. He stated that another person from the organization wanted to interview me in Philadelphia as well and asked if I could rearrange my flight plans to arrive earlier. I politely told him "no" and stated that changing anything this close to the date would be too difficult to do. I kept my flight plans the same and hoped to fit both of the interviewers in within the initial time frame. The recruiter consented and I was scheduled for back to back interviews starting at 3 p.m.

However, for the first time, I felt some hesitancy about this job. I initially pursued the position back in late June and had patiently waited for everything to progress up until now. For them to be unorganized leading up to the final interview stage was disappointing. In addition, asking me to change my flight plans last minute before the week of Thanksgiving did not sit well with me either. However, I still wanted the job and prepared for Philadelphia.

The morning of the 21st, my flight was scheduled to depart at 10:25 a.m. I had a layover in Washington, D.C. for a little over an hour. From there, I would fly into Philadelphia and arrive at 1:55 p.m., which was cutting it close to catch transportation and reach the interview location on time. However, I was not carrying any luggage and the location was only nine miles away from the airport. The only other alternative would have been catching a much earlier morning flight and having a longer layover. I rolled the dice and took the convenient risk that everything would work out fine.

The first flight to Washington, D.C. departed and arrived as scheduled. During the layover, I reviewed a couple of notes and tried to stay relaxed. As I boarded the flight to Philadelphia I got comfortable in my seat and waited for takeoff. As the time for departure passed, I grew a little concerned but figured we would be leaving momentarily. The pilot then made an announcement apologizing for the delay but stated that the delaying issue would be cleared up shortly. I felt relieved and continued to think about what was ahead and making it to the first interview on time.

Another ten minutes passed and I knew something was wrong. All of a sudden, an announcement came on for all passengers to deboard the plane! After deboarding, I knew arriving on time was in jeopardy. I emailed the recruiter and informed him of the unfortunate change of events. He was to then email the two interviewers and update them of my delay.

It took the longest time for the flight crew of the airline to say anything about what happened and when the flight to Philadelphia would depart. As I sat there in the terminal, I had second thoughts about not taking an earlier flight time that morning and how a late arrival may impact my perception with the interviewers.

Regardless, I told myself that everything happens for a reason and I tried to remain calm. The airline had to find another available plane, have it transported to the other side of the airport and then have it filled with gas and cleaned. With all that having to be done, the flight did not end up leaving until after 2 p.m.

As the plane approached Philadelphia, everything was going smoothly and I was eager to get off upon landing. Suddenly, another unforeseen event happened as a young man went into a seizure! The flight attendants remained relatively calm and asked if there were any medical professionals on board. Luckily there was a female doctor on the plane who was able to provide urgent assistance.

They covered the young man in some blankets and held onto him until the paramedics arrived. In between that time, no one was allowed to get off the plane. As I sat there and began to get frustrated, I had to catch myself. This young man's life and well-being was way more important than any job interview. Once again, I was forced to look at life from a holistic, unselfish perspective. After the paramedics made it on the plane and carried him off on a stretcher, there was a sense of relief and concern felt by everyone.

As I walked off the plane and through the airport, mentally I had already gone through a full day. Between the two flights, the delay and the seizure my mind had lost focus on the whole reason I left the house that morning - to interview for the job. I quickly caught a taxi and tried to refocus myself on the task at hand. While on the way there, the taxi driver and I conversed about the great football season the Philadelphia Eagles were having. The whole city was hoping they could continue their impressive run all the way to the Super Bowl!

I arrived at the interview location at approximately 4:20 p.m. I signed myself in and waited for the interviewers to come down. As they came through the door, they were surprisingly accompanied by another young lady who had arrived to be interviewed as well. All four of us introduced ourselves and, due to time constraints, the interviewers decided to split up with each of them interviewing one of the candidates. My interviewer was a female, the Community Development Divisional Manager, for the region I would be working in. As we began the interview, she had a copy of my resume in hand.

I initially apologized for my tardiness and I went on to say how appreciative I was to be there despite all the things that had happened. She stated that the situation with my flight was out of my control and understandable. As we talked, she spoke about what was needed to be successful in the position. She also went on to explain the hierarchy of the department and how valued input from different levels was welcomed and needed. I spoke about my core values as a person and how those values impacted my professional career. I also spoke about why the organization and this position interested me. After about forty minutes, she looked at her watch and decided it was time to conclude the interview. She provided me her business card and told me to feel free to contact her with any further questions.

We both walked over to the other side of the floor where the other interviewer and candidate were. Me and the other candidate switched places and the second interview began. The second interviewer, a man, was in charge of the whole Community Development Department. Our conversation did not last long as both the lady interviewer and I had flights to catch in less than three hours.

As the second interview concluded, all four of us decided to go across the street and catch a bite to eat. As we walked outside, it was now dark and the city had come alive! The design and the lighting of the buildings were really impressive and created an energetic atmosphere.

At dinner the male interviewer and I had a chance to converse more. The female candidate was also asked some additional questions as our competition spilled over to the dinner table. In vying to impress the interviewers, we tried to respond to their questions with valid points and solid responses. It was like a subtle game of chess being played. Once the food arrived talking became limited due to having to eat quickly. I ended up not finishing my meal and taking it to go.

As we walked out of the restaurant and down a couple of blocks, the male interviewer motioned a taxi for the female interviewer and I. Before getting in we all exchanged goodbyes and wished each other an enjoyable Thanksgiving holiday. I felt relieved that the interviews were over but could not totally relax because one of the interviewers was in the taxi with me.

"Do you mind if I finish eating my food," I asked. I would not have time to eat once I got to the airport and did not want it to be cold.

"Go ahead," she replied. We talked on a more personal level during the ride.

She was from outside of Chicago, Illinois and had been doing a lot of work related traveling for the past couple of months. With the year winding down, she looked forward to the holidays and a more relaxed work schedule. She did not have to travel far for the Thanksgiving holiday, but still had to help her mother-in-law prepare the food. I told her of my plans to head out of state for the holiday and we continued to converse about our respective families back home. As we pulled up to the airport, I got out of the taxi first and again wished her a safe flight home and a warm Thanksgiving.

I quickly made my way through check in and security and I still had thirty minutes until boarding. In deciding to walk around, I was impressed with the different venues for eating and shopping at the airport and happened to stumble upon a souvenir shop specializing in Philadelphia themed items. In thinking of my family, I bought my youngest son a souvenir sized model airplane, my oldest son a Philadelphia Eagles fidget spinner, my daughter a T-shirt and their mother two shot glasses.

I walked back to my gate with a real sense of gratitude and relief. Regardless of what came out of the interviews, I felt proud. I managed to get through this long day and leave Philadelphia with a bag of gifts and a content smile and spirit. I looked forward to returning home and getting a good night's rest. The next day would begin the holiday weekend and I was so thankful for my life and the people in it.

12.2017

month 22

After Thanksgiving I had a lot to be grateful for and the anticipation of a new job was yet another blessing. In waiting to hear back from the recruiter, I was reminded of a conversation my mother and I had over the past weekend. I told her about all that had happened and how I would be hearing something really soon about the position. She told me regardless of whether I got the job or not, the process I had undergone the past year was worth it. I had learned to be less anxious and more patient. I had also learned to trust and rely on GOD more, to understand that I did not have to figure out everything myself.

I took our conversation to heart as I waited on the news. In the meantime, the holiday season was in full effect. This year I admittedly was in better spirits looking forward to Christmas and the merriness of this time of year. Now four years old, my youngest son had a better understanding of Christmas and was excited.

"Daddy, Santa is coming and he's going to bring lots of toys," he giggled. After putting up and decorating the tree, the children were joyful and I could tell they had anticipation that this Christmas would be special.

I remember driving home on the second Monday of the month after enjoying a peaceful evening with my family. As I turned onto my street, I thought about how I would feel if I didn't get the job. I still had not heard back from the recruiter and told myself I would not act too anxious in waiting. However, I did make peace with myself that night and said, "If the answer is 'no,' I could actually deal with it." I reflected on how much I had grown to accept GOD'S way and timing, not mine.

I am glad I made peace with myself. The following morning I did receive news from the recruiter and the answer was disappointingly NO! He said the company loved my background. However, the job was offered to another candidate with a bit more experience. As I sat at my desk reading his email, I felt deeply hurt and frustrated. It was very hard and difficult to understand why GOD would allow me to be in consideration for this position, for this long, only to be denied.

Reflecting on how I initially found out about it back in June, leading all the way up to traveling to Philadelphia for the final interviews, it felt like a door had just been slammed in my face. I began to ponder what I could have done differently. Maybe if I had sacrificed more and taken an earlier flight that morning, I would not have ended up being late? Could that have played a factor in the decision? All morning I thought about all the possible reasons why they turned me down for the job.

However, during lunch, I reminded myself of what I had agreed to the night before. I would accept the "NO" and move on in FAITH that "YES" was right around the corner. By the afternoon, I felt better and my emotions calmed. I knew I had to continue to trust GOD and that this was just another test. The question became, "Can I pass it with joy in my heart?"

That evening the bitter feelings of the morning arose again as I told the mother of my children the disappointing news.

"Be patient," she replied, nonchalantly, with a shrug.

In anger and frustration I vented, "I have been patient! What do you mean be patient? What do you think I have been doing all this time? Being patient."

Surprisingly, she did not jump on the offensive for me raising my voice at her. I could tell she understood I was just venting my frustration. However, she was not about to let my negative mood ruin the peaceful one she was enjoying.

I began to think about other coworkers and people I knew who had landed other jobs over the past year and wondered why I could not accomplish the same. Was there something wrong with me? Was I not good enough?

My situation did not seem fair. I was currently employed and being underpaid. I had been underpaid for some time and the possibility of getting a well-deserved increase would not potentially happen until sometime next year. To remedy the situation, I tried to remain patient and finally found a position I thought was my long awaited open door, just to be turned back at the final stage of the hiring process. And even though GOD had shown me so much this year, I still wondered why LORD? Why LORD? Why?

Over the next few days, I built up enough courage and strength to tell my children and parents. My daughter felt sad and bad for me because I came so close. She could not understand why I did not get the job.

"Daddy, I thought this was it! I thought the company was going to hire you," she voiced.

I had promised to take my family out for a real nice dinner once I was hired - a meal where they could order whatever they wanted including dessert. My daughter understood this promise would be put on hold and wondered if it would ever come to pass.

Of course, my mother had a different response as she did not seem shocked or moved by the news. She simply stated that the job was not what GOD had planned for me to do at the time and that I was "close." I felt a little better and decided it was time for me to fully try to get over the situation and move on. As right as the opportunity may have seemed, it was not meant to be. I had to understand that the door was closed for a reason, a reason I did not understand at the time, nevertheless it was closed purposely. With Christmas less than ten days away, I decided to refocus my mind and direct it to more important matters, my family.

The timing of the disappointing news about the job being simultaneous with Christmas helped me get over the situation better. The Saturday before the glorious holiday, I remember going to my former in-laws house for dinner. It was an enjoyable time with great spirits and an atmosphere with friendly guests, some of whom I had not seen all year. It once again reminded me that life was precious.

That evening my children received some wonderful gifts. My oldest son got a VTech watch that he loved and out of excitement said was his best Christmas gift yet. My daughter received her first Bible! It was an NIV version with a brown leather cover. I was amazed that her grandparents thought to buy her such a gift! After recognizing the significance of this gift, I felt all the more thankful for all THE LORD was doing in our lives. I truly felt blessed and knew my family was blessed as well.

The next day Christmas Eve was very still and peaceful. The weather was barely below freezing with a lot of wet snow. It made the cars sparkle and the streets appear gleaming white. As I drove around that evening, for the first time in a long time, I got excited about the white Christmas and all the beautiful scenery. Christmas Day was even better, as this year there were ample gifts for the kids to unwrap and enjoy. They all got new characters for the Lego Dimensions game they were now playing on the PlayStation. Combined with the other gifts from their grandparents, this Christmas was a special one. Reflecting back from a year ago, it was a big turnaround in the amount and type of gifts they received.

The crazy thing was I was not making any more money. However, somehow my children enjoyed a plentiful Christmas. I thought to myself how my mother was right. I did not have to carry the burden of figuring out and doing everything myself. GOD would provide in some way, shape or form. My personal financial blessing would come. I just had to remain patient in faith. Around this time, the hit gospel song *Won't He Do It* by Koryn Hawthorne came on the radio daily. That song was one of my favorites and inspired me every time I heard it. Despite the setbacks I had encountered, I still had to be determined to believe HE would still do it for me!

During the last weekend of the year, the mother of my children celebrated her birthday. This year, I actually took the time to plan out something to make her evening special. During the many years we had known each other, I did not always take her birthday to heart as I should have. As I got older, my birthday had become less significant to me. And as a result, I did not always deem this noteworthy event to be as special in the lives of others. This was a mistake I made and I wanted to be more corrective in my actions.

We went out to dinner at a restaurant she had been asking to go to for months. We sat at a table by a window, not far from a fireplace. Upon the waitress greeting us for the evening, we were both treated to a complimentary glass of champagne and the mother of my children received a red rose. As we sipped our champaign, she opened her gifts which were all arranged in a box I had decorated inside with tissue paper and confetti. She received some pumpkin spice flavored lip balm, an Amazon gift card, Trident chewing gum, an aromatherapy candle, scented plug in air freshener and hand soap from Bath and Body Works, along with a 3.4 ounce bottle of Chanel Allure perfume.

As dinner arrived at our table, she felt happy. She thanked me for making the extra effort to make her smile.

"You really put some thought into this, didn't you?" she surprisingly said.

I could tell it meant a lot to her and it was a great way to cap off a year full of ups and downs, with some victories along the way. As we were enjoying dinner, it began to snow heavily outside. I drove my car which was smaller and less equipped for heavy snowfall. As we got on the freeway headed home the snowfall created scary, white out conditions. Most cars moved at a snail's pace as snow covered the lines separating the freeway lanes. Even worse, snow kept falling making it hard to keep the front windshield defrosted.

I tried to keep my mind totally focused on the road as my car began to slide when I accelerated. I had been in my fair share of snow storms but this one had me frightened. The roads were so slippery and visibility was bad. Plus to top everything off, my gas tank was on "E". In my mind, I kicked myself for not getting some gas earlier. Fearing I would run out of gas, I decided I would veer right at an upcoming fork in the freeway then stop at an exit on the other side. But, it was so hard to see and drive I wondered if we would make it. My car continued to slide even going at a low speed and I actually contemplated pulling over, putting my hazard lights on and waiting until the snow lightened up. However, we could not be stuck in a snowstorm with no gas. We also risked someone rear ending us due to low visibility.

Then amazingly, out of nowhere, came a light grey snow plow truck in the lane to the right of us! The truck with rear fluorescent orange and green lights cleared a visible path for us to get to the nearest exit. I quickly acknowledged this timely blessing and followed the truck off the freeway. The truck led us down the exit ramp where just a short right turn away was a gas station. As I filled up my car, I thanked GOD for that truck coming right at that time and directing us. I cleared off the front windshield and let the car and myself recuperate for fifteen minutes.

When we got back on the freeway, it was a 180 degree difference on the other side of the fork. It was still snowing but the traffic was less stop and go, moving faster. Due to being able to maintain a constant speed, my car did not struggle with sliding and the remaining voyage home was a lot smoother than the beginning. As we closed in on our destination, I thought about how this trip reminded me of my life the past twenty-two months. Starting out the journey was shaky and I was sliding, unsure at first if I would make it or not. However, it got smoother as time passed. Eventually, I too would make it to my destination just as the car did that night.

As the year came to a close, this was my attitude going into 2018. Despite the setbacks I had encountered, I remained determined to believe HE would still do it for me!

KEY VERSES

As it is written,

"Cast not away therefore your confidence, which hath great recompense of reward. For ye have need of patience, that, after ye have done the will of God, ye might receive the promise. For yet a little while, and HE that shall come will come, and will not tarry. Now the just shall live by faith: but if any man draw back, my soul shall have no pleasure in him. But we are not of them who draw back unto perdition; but of them that believe to the saving of the soul."

Hebrews 10: 35-39

"Trust in the Lord with all thine heart; and lean not unto thine own understanding."

Proverbs 3:5

01.2018

month 23

Another New Year arrived and on the very first day we celebrated my daughter's eleventh birthday. Family came over for late morning brunch and everyone discussed what they did the night before. The food was exceptional and the mood was upbeat. We played games, sang songs and really enjoyed each other. The following day was my daughter's actual birthday! We went to the shopping mall and she was allowed to venture off on her own with a friend for over an hour. With her cell phone handy, it felt like she was becoming a teenager. I realized she was getting older and was no longer my little baby girl.

During January, I tried to keep my mind moving forward and not regressing on the past. What happened had to stay in the rear view, with my mind now focused on the future. Being a new year, I believed new experiences were in store. The first new experience of the year happened on the 9th, surprisingly right at home. I was returning to the main house after dropping my daughter off at a friend's house. To my surprise, the mother of my children was playing gospel music loudly. She was cheerfully smiling while moving and dancing to Kirk Franklin songs.

The amazing thing about this was I had just prayed that morning asking GOD for the important people in my life to begin to understand how much of a central part HE needed to be in their lives. I had been praying this prayer for the mother of my children for some time, especially during the last twenty months. To witness her listening to Kirk Franklin and being enthused and moved by gospel music was a beautiful thing. I really made me feel happy and joyful inside.

The mother of my children was not a stranger to gospel music or church. In her youth, she attended church regularly through her high school years. Like me, her attendance veered off during college and we had not been serious church goers since the early years of our marriage. However, I was grateful and remembered the Bible verse of *Romans 10:17*, "So then faith cometh by hearing, and hearing by the word of God." That word could come through a preacher, a song or the Bible. It could be delivered in a variety of different ways. If GOD was using Kirk Franklin to minister to the mother of my children's soul, I was all for it!

In turn, GOD ministered to me a day later on the way home from work. As I listened to the radio, the Willie Moore Jr. show was on. I typically listened to the show on my way home and that day Willie had a message for me. His message was *Man's Rejection was GOD's Protection.* Of course, this led me to think about being turned down for the job last month. How even though I felt so rejected at the time, maybe it was for my own good and protection.

While at work the next day, I happened to stumble across news online announcing that President Trump planned on making major changes to the Community Reinvestment Act. This act regulated lending that banks did in low to moderate income communities. I would have been working under this act if hired by the community bank. Any changes to the lending regulations could have affected me in that position.

After reading this news it really made me think about Willie's message. I realized that sometimes you have to thank THE LORD for closed doors, for desires of yours HE chooses not to grant at a particular time. In acknowledging GOD's infinite wisdom, HE could foresee situations I couldn't. Thus HE could shield me from potential harm. Going forward, I tried to keep this thought close to my mind.

Over the weekend, we went to *Disney on Ice* and enjoyed the best seats ever! We originally were supposed to attend the show the night before but, due to bad weather, decided to call the box office and see if we could attend the following evening. They granted our request and ended up giving us better seats. We ended up sitting on the floor level, row four to be exact! We had been to many Disney events over the years but never had seats this close.

As I sat enjoying the show, I tried to stay in the moment. Being so close, it was easy to take in all the bright lights, scenery and characters. The atmosphere was magical! As I sat there, I locked in on the eyes of my children and their smiles and could feel the wonderful vibes. My youngest son wore the biggest smile since *Moana* was one of the themes and he loved the songs from the movie. I was sure the mother of my children had not paid the full price for the seats we received that night. Nevertheless, we enjoyed the favor with hopes that a new year would continue to usher in more unmerited blessings in our direction.

As the month ended, my oldest son started playing basketball. One Saturday before his game started, there was another game in progress. The score of the game was close. In the final minutes, you could feel the competition intensifying. The yellow team ended up coming from behind to tie the game.

The leader of this team was a young man who willed his team into overtime by hitting three straight jump shots within the last minutes of the game. All three shots were from the right wing of the basket as this young man was fearless and determined. He meticulously would dribble the ball to his favorite spot on the floor and once he got there he would shoot. His determination to score was stronger than the defense trying to stop him.

This young man's heroics continued in overtime as his team was down two points with under a minute left. He somehow got to his spot on the right wing again and hit another shot to retie the game! I said to myself, "How did the opposing team allow him to get to his favorite spot and get the shot off?" Now tied again with fourteen seconds left, I thought for sure the game would go into a second overtime.

With one final chance, one of the players from the opposing team dribbled the ball down the right side of the court and threw up a shot that missed badly. The shot was an air ball that sailed completely over the rim. Luckily, one of his teammates was able to pick the ball up and as he stood there, the restless crowd yelled, "Shoot!" The young man threw the shot up and it went in all net! He was mobbed by his teammates and ended up being the hero of the game.

After basketball that afternoon, I reflected on the events of the day. It reminded me that new beginnings and new things were happening all the time. I could not get discouraged about my current situation and how things appeared to not be changing. I did not know when I would get the ball and have an opportunity to shoot my shot. The boy that hit the game winning shot that day did not have a chance to think about what he was doing. With time running out, he shot the ball and made his opportunity all net as his chance for success seemed to naturally unfold.

Just like the boy, I did not know when my opportunity would come. Life was full of possibilities and, from one day to the next, I did not know what could happen or how my life or others would be impacted. However, the one thing I swore to do was to continue enjoying everyday life and the joys and appreciation it brought. The small things like watching those kids play basketball and seeing the heroics they displayed inspired me. Like a lot of other parents in the stands, I enjoyed watching the youth basketball games more than the NBA. It was a great way to spend a couple hours on a Saturday afternoon.

02.2018

month 24

The month of February was a historic one that brought changes in everyday life. It featured the release of the blockbuster movie *Black Panther* as I was privileged to see this record breaking film with my family. While in the movie, we received the sad news that the mother of my children's grandmother, Ms. Kennedy, died. She was the matriarch of that side of the family and her passing signified a transitioning. She had been sick for a while and everyone recognized this day would come. However, it was like a giant had fallen. She commanded that much respect from the people she interacted with.

At her funeral, I was more emotional than usual. I prided myself on not crying much at funerals because I viewed them as a celebration of life, not an event to mourn. I knew Ms. Kennedy was a devoted Christian and her eternal fate was in heaven with THE LORD! However, I did shed some tears and tried to remember her life and what she meant to the family. It reminded me that no matter how larger than life any one of us may seem, one day we all would die and our life on Earth would cease to exist.

Even though my own death seemed too soon to imagine, it had become all the more real to me that one day I would also be in a casket surrounded by my family and close friends. I understood with all the craziness going on, tomorrow was not promised. With the tragic, monumental high school shooting happening in Parkland, Florida earlier in the month, life seemed that much more precious to me and death that more real. As I held my oldest son in my lap at the funeral, I realized that in the end love is what mattered most above all else.

The month also featured some very promising moments. Moments that provided me great encouragement and gratitude going forward. The first came on the night of President's Day. As I left the main house, I could not help but notice the extremely calm mood. The mother of my children was relaxing on the couch, watching reruns of *Little House on the Prairie*. She had a grin on her face and seemed totally at peace with the world. Reflecting back months ago, this was not foreseeable as she was so stressed about so many things. Her mood showed how far she had come and how much GOD had intervened in her life.

My youngest son was in the other room quietly watching television and the two oldest were already in bed. After leaving that night, I thanked GOD for how HE had kept and sustained us. Despite all the ups and downs of the past twenty-four months, my family was blessed to still be living in the same house in the same quiet neighborhood. I was in awe of how far GOD had brought us along this journey. HE had truly been good and kept HIS hands around us.

Another moment was three days later when my oldest son received a perfect score of forty-five points on his fifth module math test! I had been ragging on him for most of the school year about his math grade. He started off the year slowly but since then had gained momentum as I constantly reminded him to stay focused in class. For him to perform the way he did on this latest test was amazing and showed his journey of progress! Personally, it was a huge boost as it made me realize he actually was listening to what I was telling him.

As a parent, sometimes you think your teaching is in vain and that your children are not listening. However, I realized kids listen more than you think. Even though it may not always show and they may seem to not be interested in what you are trying to get across to them, your teaching will eventually sink in and make a difference. Like prayer, sometimes results may take longer to show up but they will come! My son's changed performance in math was a sure sign to me that GOD could still intervene in situations where I needed change through prayer.

THE LORD reinforced this thought to me on the last day of the month. Midday, I was at work in my office, when I suddenly heard a man's voice. He was singing the renowned Sam Cooke song, *A Change Is Gonna Come*. Something about the way that man sang the song, drew me to eventually get up out of my chair, walk out of my office and down the hallway to see him perform. When I got there, I was fortunate to catch the last minute of his performance and wished I had arrived sooner.

The man sang the song with so much emotion and conviction. Since he was singing at the end of the Black History event going on, no one from his intended audience seemed to be paying him any attention. People had already left their assigned seats and walked around networking as the event concluded. This was sad because his performance was passionate and moving. It resonated with my spirit that change was coming. I had been waiting on my change and knew it was on the way. The best was yet to come!

KEY VERSES

As it is written,

"And now abideth faith, hope, charity, these three; but the greatest of these is charity."
I Corinthians 13:13

"Train up a child in the way he should go: and when he is old, he will not depart from it."
Proverbs 22:6

BONUS MONTH

MARCH 2018 AND BEYOND

On the first night of March, there was a winter storm approaching so I didn't spend a lot of time at the main house. I stopped by after work to eat dinner and briefly see everybody. I remember my children being in a really good mood. Their mother had bought them some new Lego Dimensions toys, so they were all smiles.

After dinner, she put on some music and my children began dancing. As I watched the three of them in the family room having a joyful time, their laughter and giggling reminded me of the blessings in my life. My children were doing well in school and they were happy and healthy. Most of all they knew they were loved!

A week later, my daughter graduated from the Drug Abuse Resistance Education (D.A.R.E.) program at her school. Initially, when I received the invitation to the ceremony, I was surprised and unaware that the D.A.R.E. program was still being taught. I gladly attended the graduation and had a chance to hear the D.A.R.E. Officer speak on how the program had evolved over the years to now being more focused on disciplining children to make good, smart decisions.

I realized my daughter was at the point of her life where decision-making would start becoming important and I felt truly fortunate that she received this type of mentoring at school. You could tell from the way the D.A.R.E. Officer interacted with the kids that a bond had formed over the course of the program. That bond was part of the overall village raising my daughter and others her age.

As the month rolled along, I remember playing a board game with my two oldest children one Sunday afternoon. I had not won at this particular game in a while, as we played it a couple weeks back and both of my children beat me. Lately, the game seemed to be kinder to them. However, I felt optimistic and accepted their challenge to play.

This particular day we played two rounds and I happened to win both! In the first round, I seamlessly won as my luck could not have been better. In the second round, my repeat victory was almost as seamless as the first and my daughter was surprised.

"Daddy, looks like your luck is finally turning around. It's about time for your money train to come," she said.

Later that afternoon, after dropping my daughter off at volleyball camp, I could not help but remember what she said about my luck changing. It prompted me to remember a message that I just heard earlier that morning over the radio. The pastor preached out of *Luke 22:31,32* in recapping the story of JESUS telling Peter that Satan desired to have him and sift him as wheat. However, JESUS told Peter that HE had prayed for him that his faith failed not.

I took this passage to heart and looked back at my experience over the past twenty-four months. I was proud to say my faith had not failed. Even though some things still had not come to pass that I had been hoping and praying for, my faith still had not wavered. I still believed GOD knew of everything that had been and was going on in my life and that HE was in charge of my breakthrough and where my answers would come from.

Over the past twenty-four months, my faith had become a constant, steadfast force in my life. However, it started off not certain and shaky. Over time, it developed and produced endurance and rest. It's development was founded on and continually strengthened by the WORD OF GOD and the encounters I faced and overcame.

In recapping the last twenty-four months, I had endured many things. From the dissolution of my marriage, to financial turmoil and eventually filing for bankruptcy, to dealing with multiple health issues and surgeries with the mother of my children, to almost losing my house to foreclosure and dealing with closed doors and unanswered prayers. It had been the most trying time of my life.

At times it felt like I was hung up by a chain being whipped. I felt myself agonizing internally. Being hung up and whipped, Satan had been trying to get me to submit to life and the things happening to me. I was being tested to not submit and give in but to build up a tolerance for the lashings. As much as I went through, I would not trade my experience for anything, not anything. Time and time again, GOD revealed HIMSELF and provided!

HE always did so, seemingly in ways that had nothing directly to do with me or required any additional effort on my part. My steady efforts were focused on prayer, staying in HIS WORD and continually trying to put my best foot forward each day. In learning to enjoy everyday life, I eventually began to see my glass as half full and not half empty.

More importantly, along with faith, I developed more empathy and a deeper awareness for the well-being of others. I learned to be more selfless, to pray more for others and be less judgmental. To sum it all up, I learned what it means to **LOVE**.

I did not have a true understanding of the meaning of love before, even while I was married. Like a lot of people, I would use the word too loosely without fully grasping what I was actually talking about. After my twenty-four month experience, I truly understood why GOD was LOVE and why as "Professing Christians" we are called to love GOD and one another.

As a Professing Christian Man, who has gone through the experience documented in this book, I have a true obligation going forward to be the person GOD has willed me to be. This challenge will require GOD to continue to do a great work in me. To further evolve from being a Professing Christian Man to a Committed One. Regardless of what comes my way, I know GOD will continue to uphold me even in the toughest times.

In concluding this memoir, I would like to recognize and encourage anyone who is going through their own wilderness experience. I pray and hope that your faith does not fail along your journey. I need you to understand and realize that Almighty GOD is doing a great work in you. That HE understands and is aware of everything going on in your life. I encourage you to be patient, to stay in prayer and to press on in faith and not become weary in well doing. You will enjoy better times and see brighter days!

I would also like to recognize and encourage all those in the BODY OF CHRIST who minister to the BODY. No matter your role, whether you are a singer, minister, spiritual counselor or radio personality. If you edify, build up and develop the BODY, please know that your work is invaluable. I can't mention how many times during my experience that a song or something I heard someone say uplifted me. This encouragement continually strengthened my belief and helped keep me going in the right direction.

As Christians, we are all called to witness to non-believers and win souls to JESUS CHRIST. A lot of attention and emphasis is given to this commission. However, I also believe that it is just as important to effectively continue to minister and develop the BODY, so as disciples we can become better fishers of men and women.

Finally, I would like to put a call out and challenge to all the Professing Christian Men. For us to be better Fathers, better Husbands and better Men. We can choose to exhibit more grace, humility and love and still be strong Men for our families, communities and churches. Just because you exhibit these characteristics does not make you a weak or lesser Man. It makes you a Man with the heart of GOD. As Professing Christian Men, I believe we must learn how to continually develop and exhibit these characteristics, so we can directly influence those around us in a more effective, powerful way!

MAY JEHOVAH GOD CONTINUE TO BLESS US ALL

CONCLUDING KEY VERSES

As it is written,

"Being confident of this very thing, that he which hath begun a good work in you will perform it until the day of Jesus Christ."
Philippians 1:6

"And let us not be weary in well doing: for in due season we shall reap, if we faint not."
Galatians 6:9

"This is my commandment, That ye love one another, as I have loved you."
John 15:12

ACKNOWLEDGEMENTS

I would like to thank the characters and people mentioned in this book. The information enclosed in it is very personal and without your support and cooperation this project would not have been possible.

Also, thank you to all the singers of Gospel music. Growing up, I was not a big listener of this genre. Besides hearing the choir at church, I rarely heard it otherwise. During my teenage years, I began to see more gospel artists like BeBe and CeCe Winans, Kirk Franklin, Yolanda Adams and Donnie McClurkin appear on television and gain more commercial exposure. At the time, they seemed to bring a more modern day feel to the genre as I knew it.

However, during my twenty-four month experience, Gospel music became a huge inspiration in my life! I could name quite a few artists, I would often hear while riding in my car, who poured into my spirit daily. Thus, I will continue to listen to Gospel music and I want to encourage all the Gospel artists out there to continue your ministry of edifying the BODY OF CHRIST!

CALL TO ACTION LETTER

Dear Reader:

Thank You for taking the time to read this book. I truly put my heart and soul into it. Hopefully, you enjoyed reading about my experience and journey. Hopefully, it blessed your life!

I would love to hear your feedback. Please leave a review on Amazon and/or Goodreads about this title. Feel free to request it at your local library. Also, tell your family and friends about it! Word of Mouth and reviews are so essential to independent authors. I can also be reached at my website www.byrondemery.com.

Sincerely,

Byron Demery

www.ingramcontent.com/pod-product-compliance
Lightning Source LLC
Chambersburg PA
CBHW071925290426
44110CB00013B/1481